FOR ORGANS, PIANOS & ELECTRONIC KEYBOARDS

E-Z PLAY® TODAY

001

FAVORITE SONGS
WITH 3 CHORDS

P9-DMV-586

2	ALOHA OE
4	AMAZING GRACE
6	AMERICA
8	AURA LEE
9	BARCAROLLE
10	BEAUTIFUL DREAMER
14	BLOW THE MAN DOWN
12	BLUE DANUBE WALTZ
16	CAISSONS GO ROLLING ALONG, THE
18	CAN CAN POLKA
20	CHIAPANECAS
22	CIELITO LINDO
24	CLEMENTINE
26	DRINK TO ME ONLY WITH THINE EYES
28	DU, DU LIEGST MIR IM HERZEN
30	FASCINATION
32	FOR HE'S A JOLLY GOOD FELLOW
34	FRANKIE AND JOHNNY
36	HE'S GOT THE WHOLE WORLD IN HIS HANDS
38	HOME SWEET HOME
40	JUST A CLOSER WALK WITH THEE
42	KUMBAYA
44	LONDONDERRY AIR
15	LULLABY
47	MARIANNE
48	MARINE'S HYMN
50	MICHAEL, ROW THE BOAT ASHORE
52	MY OLD KENTUCKY HOME
54	ODE TO JOY
57	OH! SUSANNA
60	OH, THEM GOLDEN SLIPPERS
62	ON TOP OF OLD SMOKY
64	OVER THE WAVES
66	RED RIVER VALLEY
68	SHENANDOAH
70	TA-RA-RA-BOOM-DE-AY
73	WABASH CANNON BALL
80	WHEN THE SAINTS GO MARCHING IN
76	YANKEE DOODLE
78	YELLOW ROSE OF TEXAS

ISBN 978-0-7935-2198-2

HAL•LEONARD®
CORPORATION
7777 W. BLUEMOUND RD. P.O. BOX 13819 MILWAUKEE, WI 53213

E-Z Play ® TODAY Music Notation © 1975 HAL LEONARD PUBLISHING CORPORATION
Copyright ©1993 by HAL LEONARD PUBLISHING CORPORATION
International Copyright Secured   All Rights Reserved

Aloha Oe

Registration 2
Rhythm: Swing

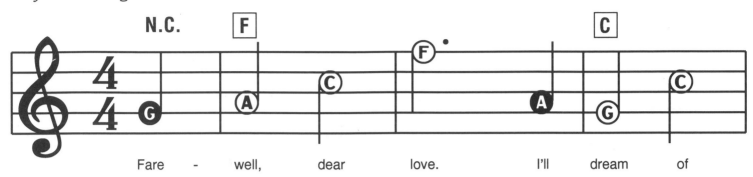

Fare - well, dear love. I'll dream of

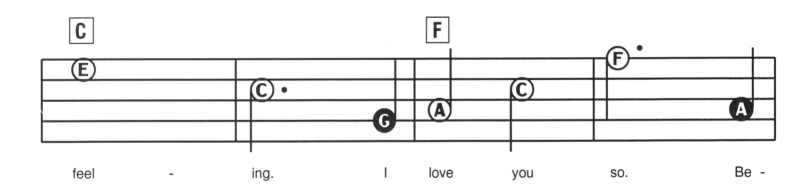

you. No pass - ing grief is this my heart is

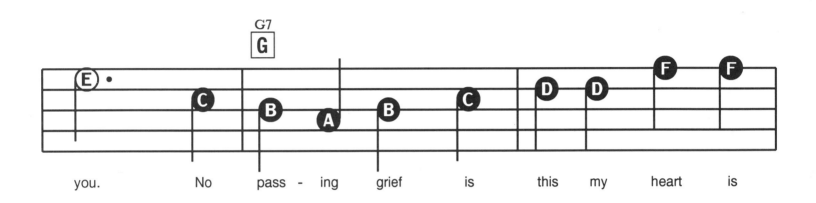

feel - ing. I love you so. Be -

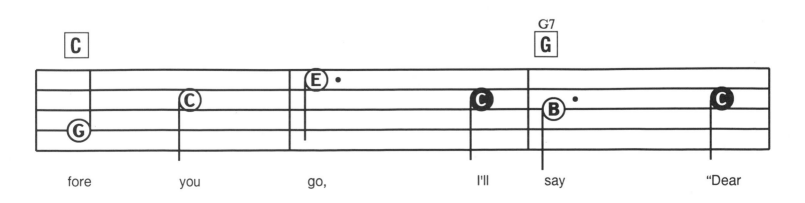

fore you go, I'll say "Dear

3

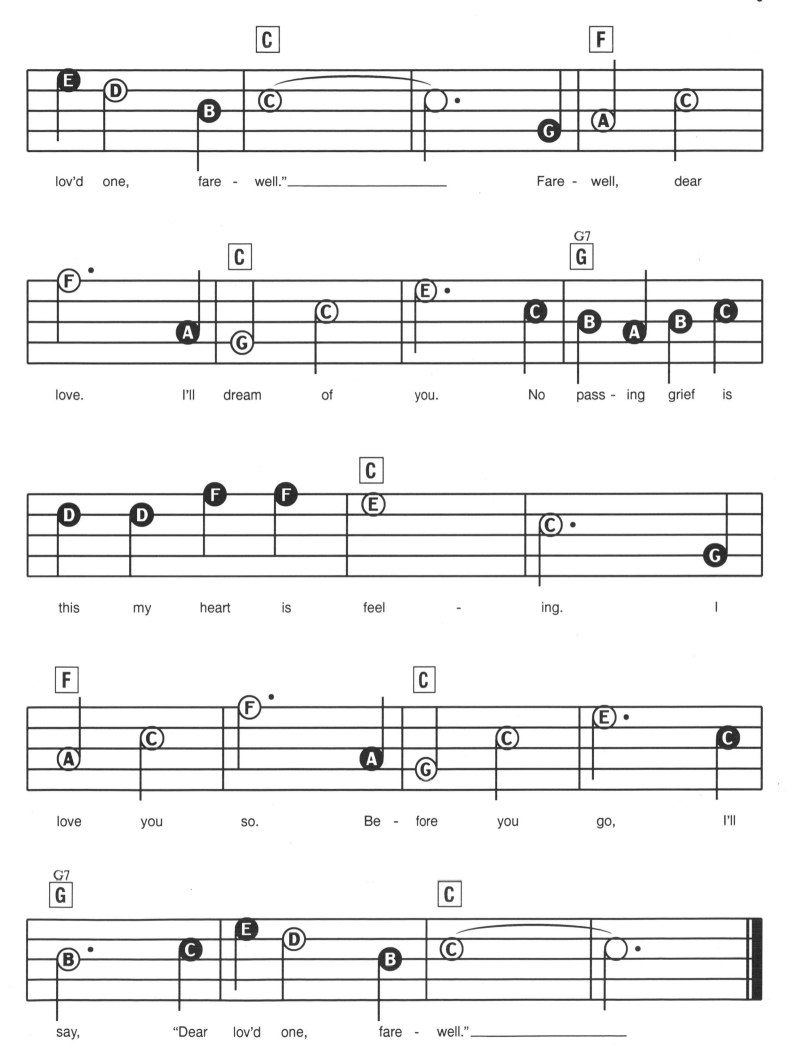

Amazing Grace

Registration 2
Rhythm: Waltz

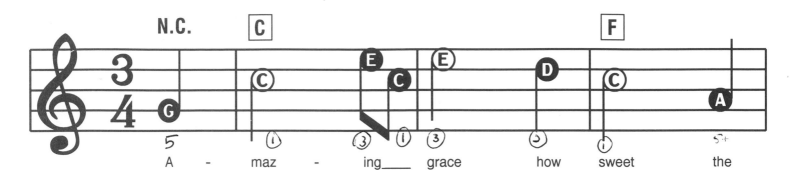

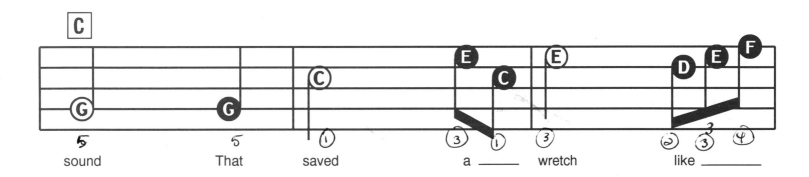

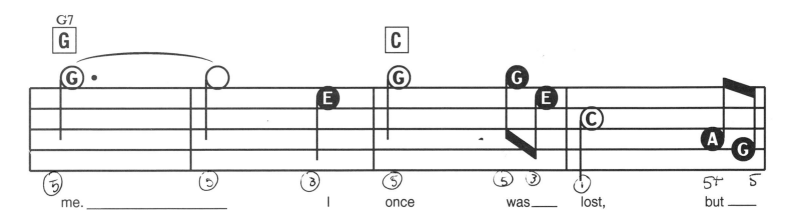

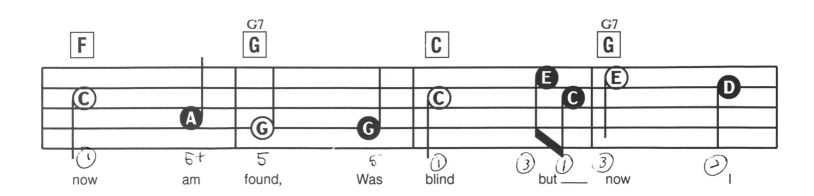

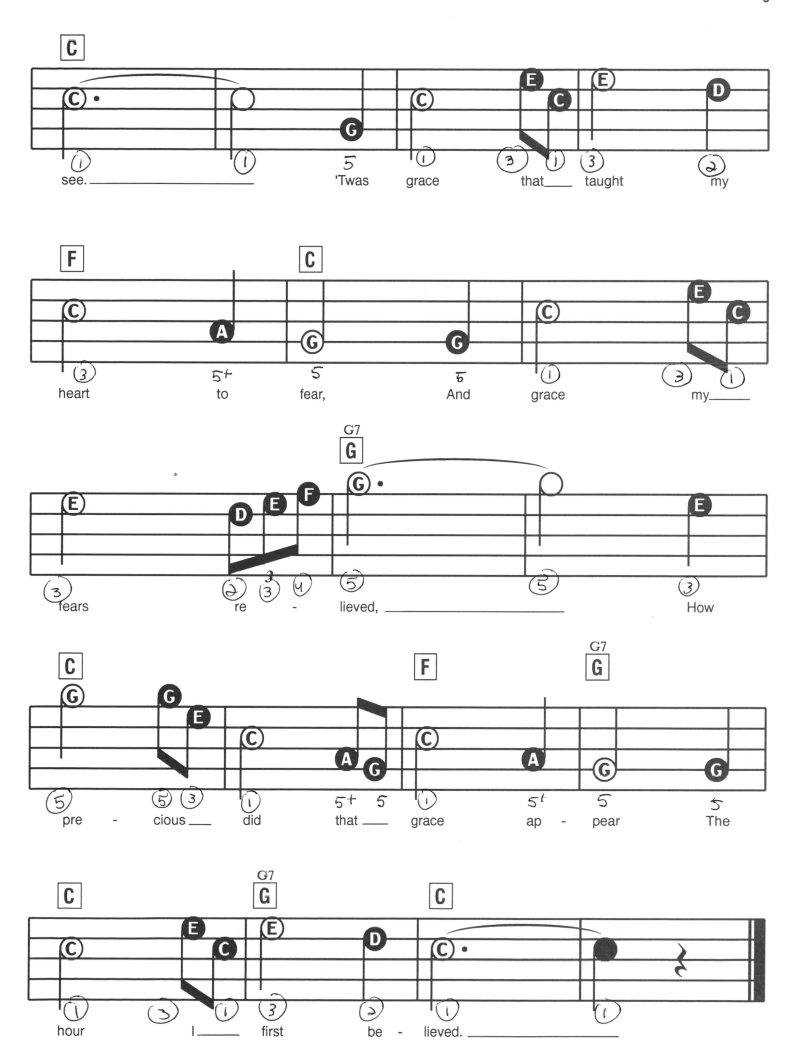

America

Registration 5
Rhythm: Waltz or none

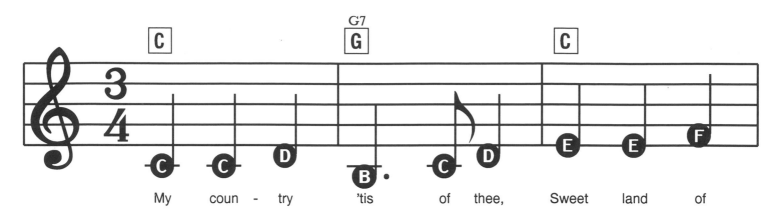

My coun - try 'tis of thee, Sweet land of

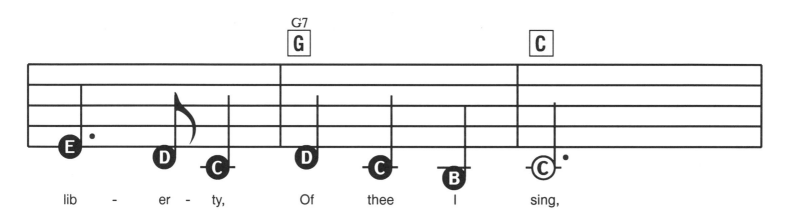

lib - er - ty, Of thee I sing,

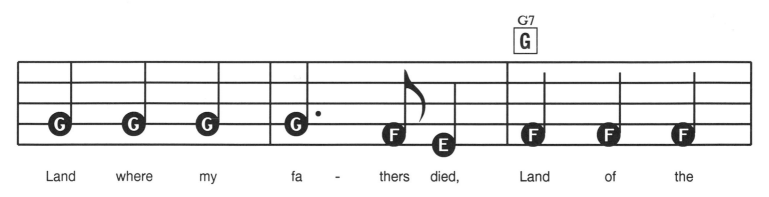

Land where my fa - thers died, Land of the

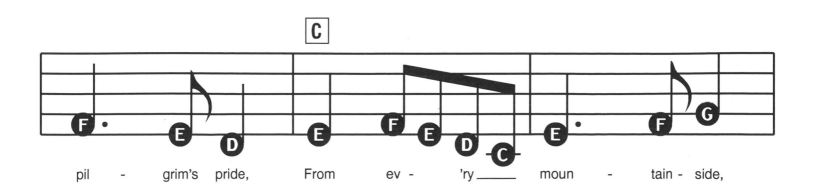

pil - grim's pride, From ev - 'ry____ moun - tain - side,

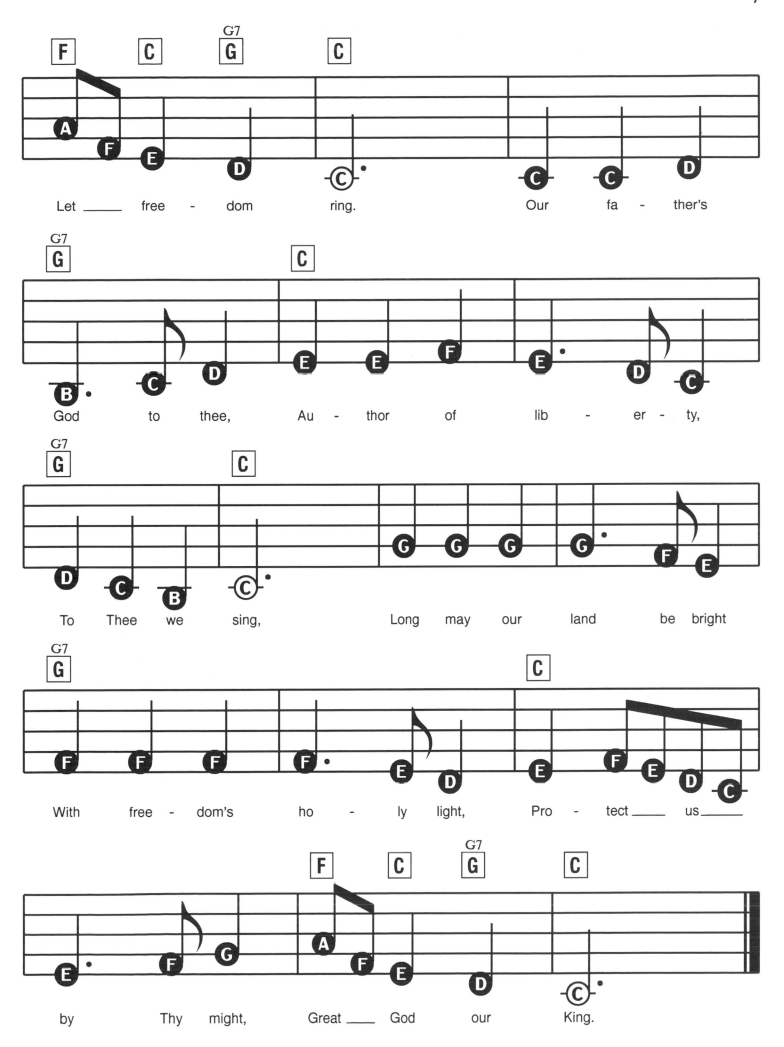

Aura Lee

Registration 3
Rhythm: Swing

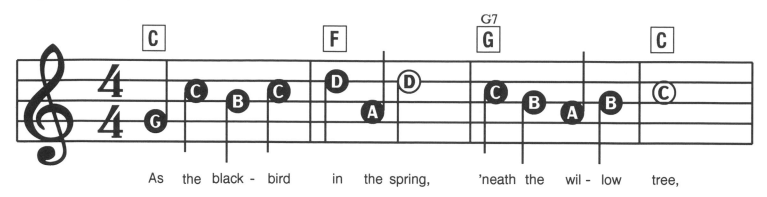

As the black - bird   in the spring,   'neath the wil - low   tree,

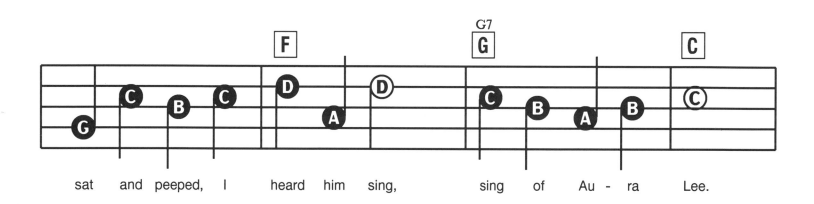

sat and peeped, I   heard him sing,   sing of Au - ra   Lee.

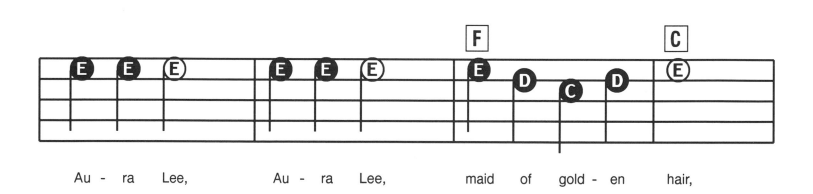

Au - ra Lee,   Au - ra Lee,   maid of gold - en   hair,

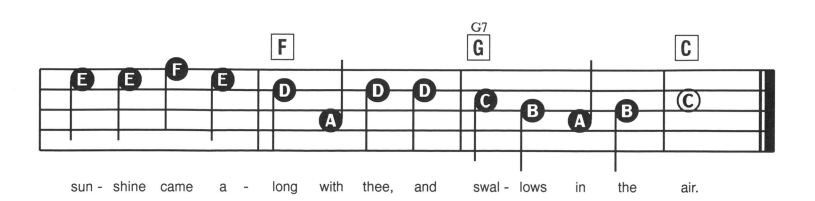

sun - shine came a - long with thee, and   swal - lows in the   air.

Barcarolle

Registration 4
Rhythm: Waltz

Offenbach

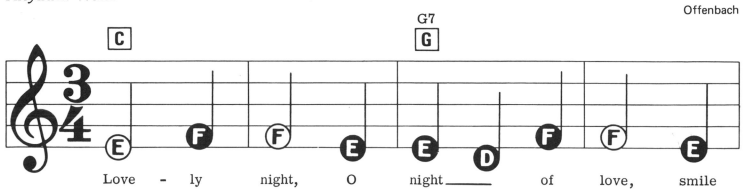

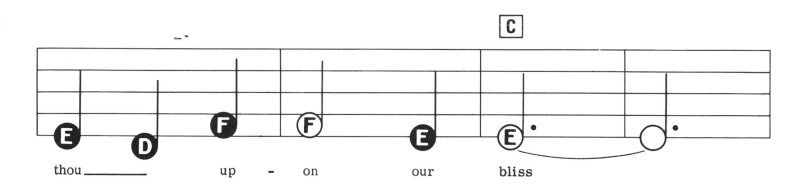

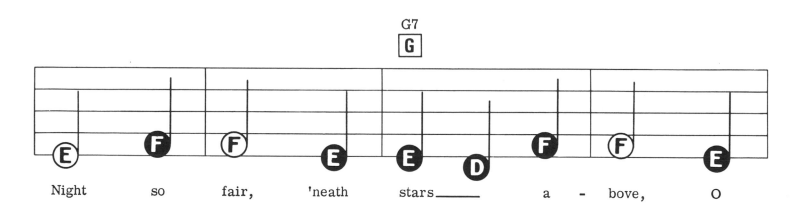

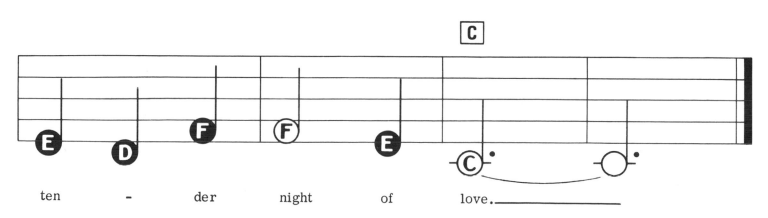

Beautiful Dreamer

Registration 5
Rhythm: Waltz

Stephen Collins Foster

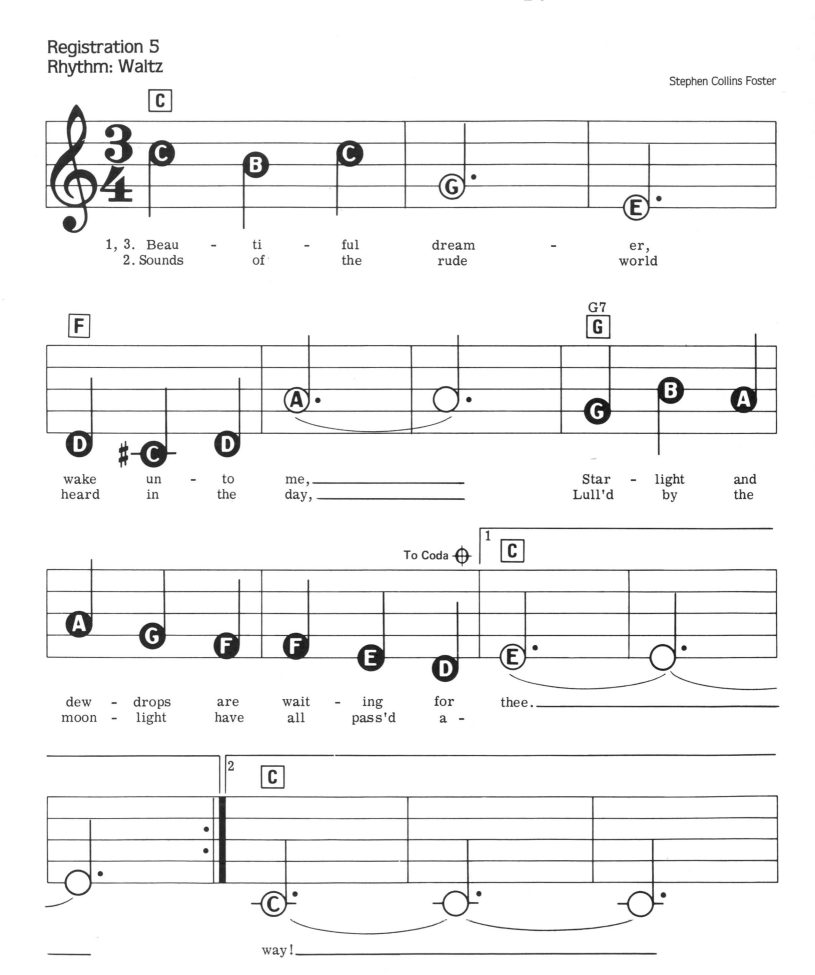

11

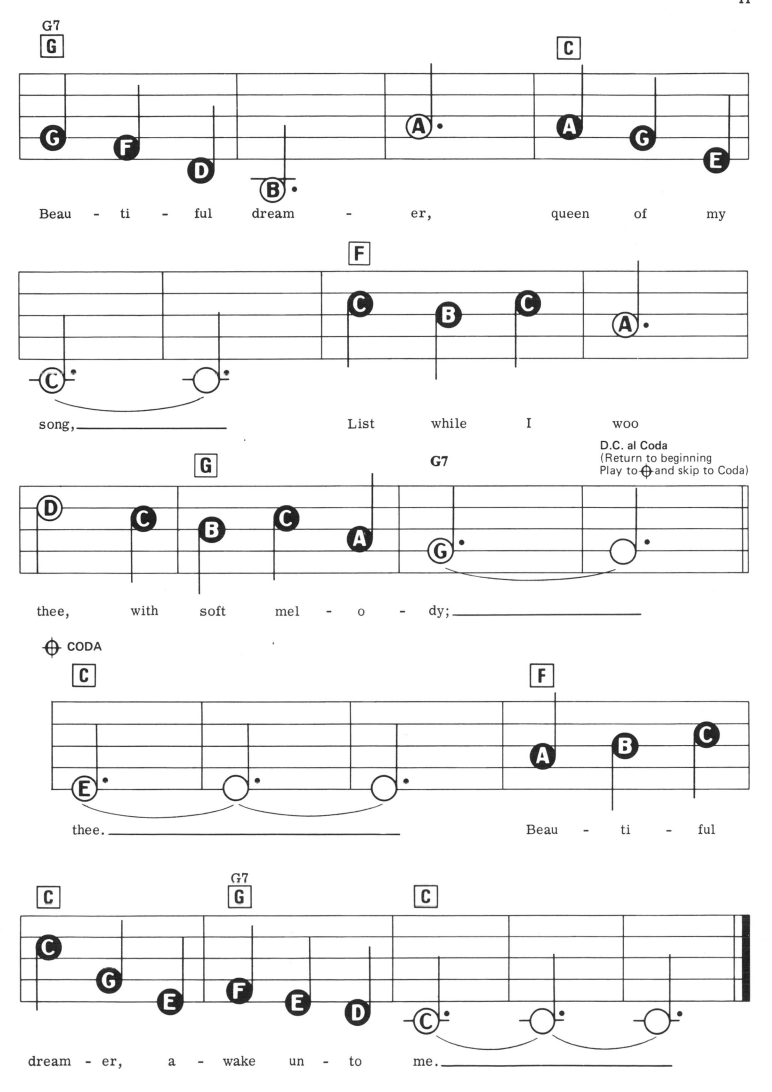

Blue Danube Waltz

Registration 2
Rhythm: Waltz

Johann Strauss

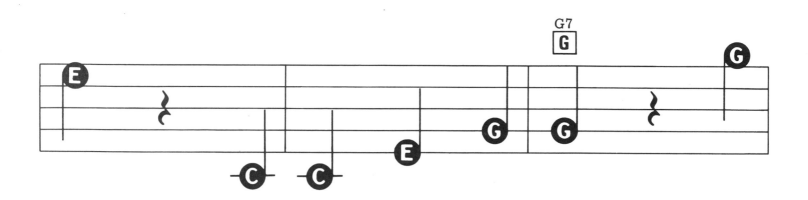

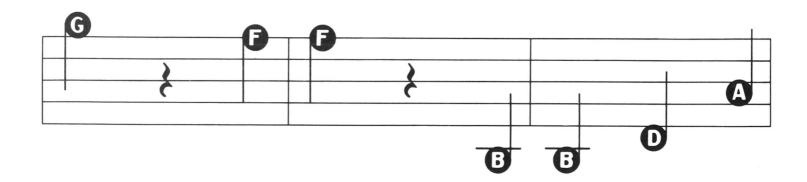

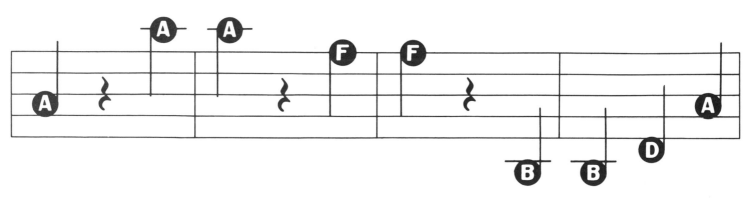

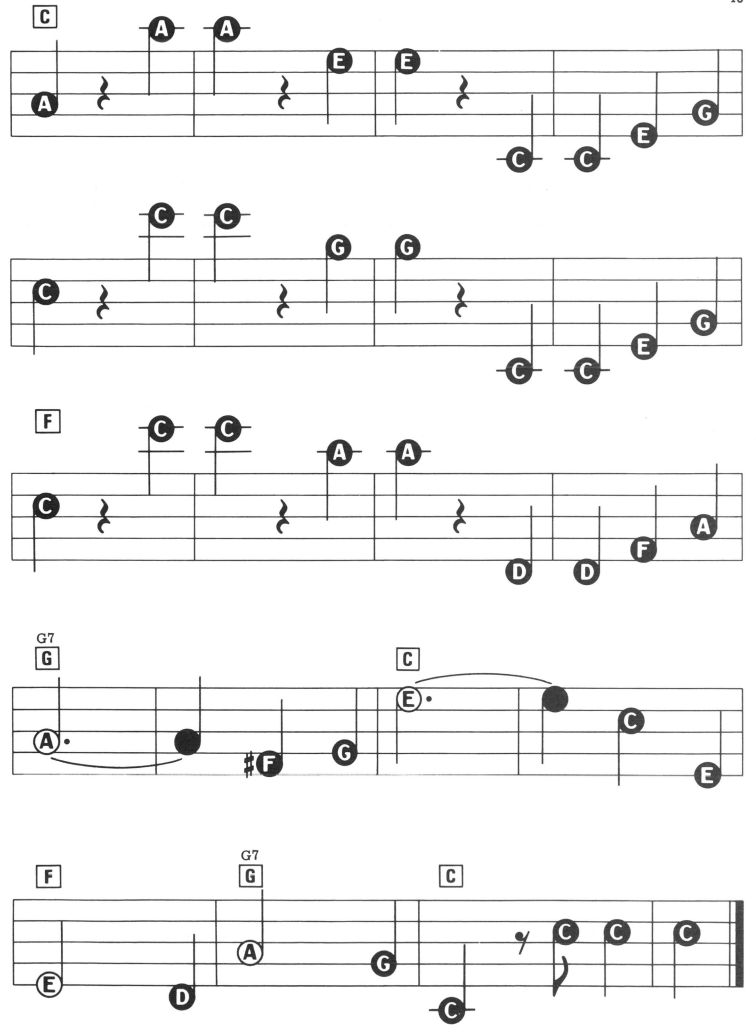

Blow The Man Down

Registration 9
Rhythm: Waltz

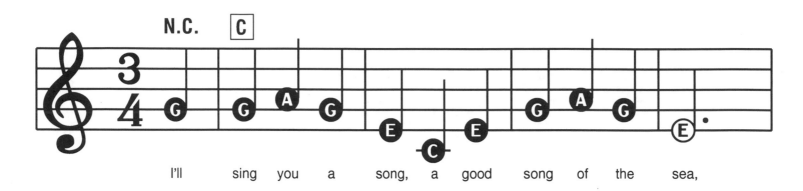

I'll sing you a song, a good song of the sea,

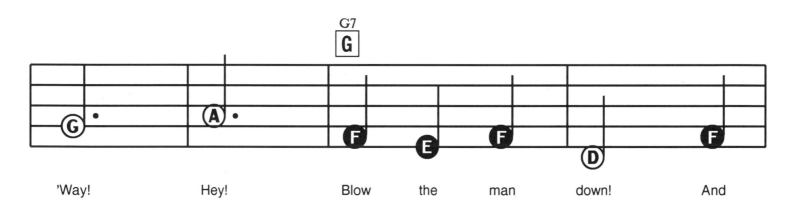

'Way! Hey! Blow the man down! And

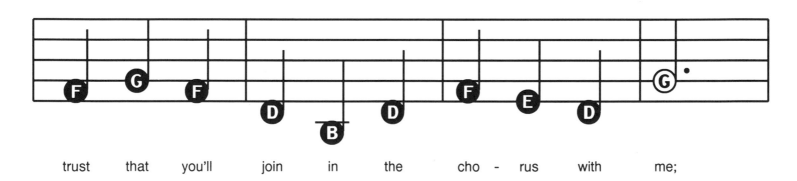

trust that you'll join in the cho - rus with me;

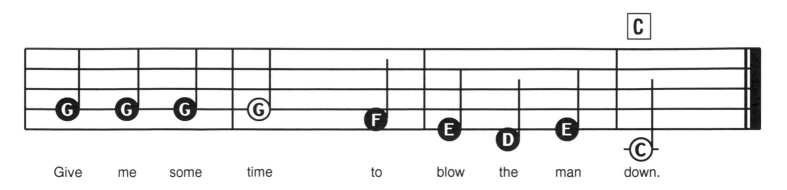

Give me some time to blow the man down.

Lullaby

Registration 1
Rhythm: Waltz

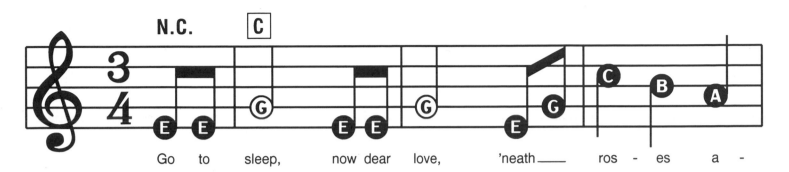

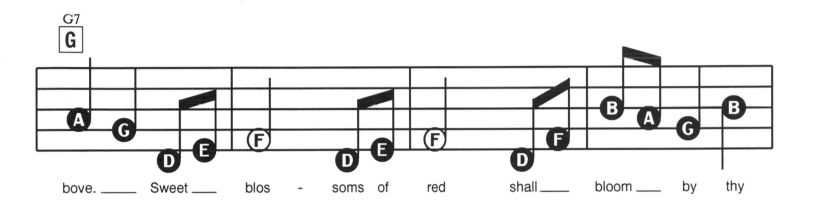

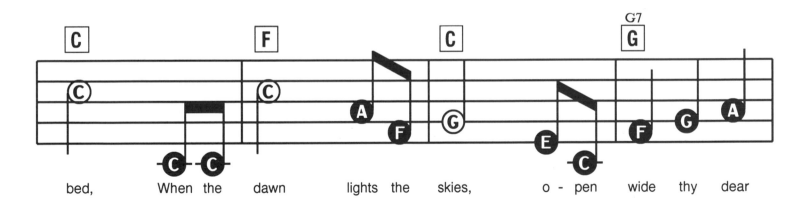

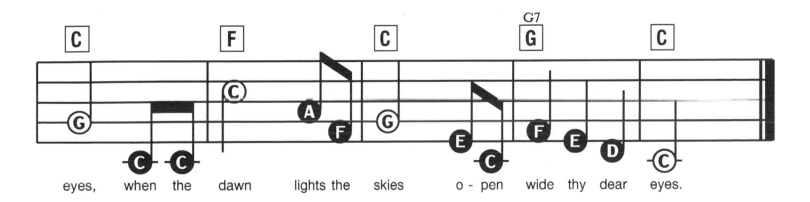

The Caissons Go Rolling Along

Registration 2
Rhythm: March

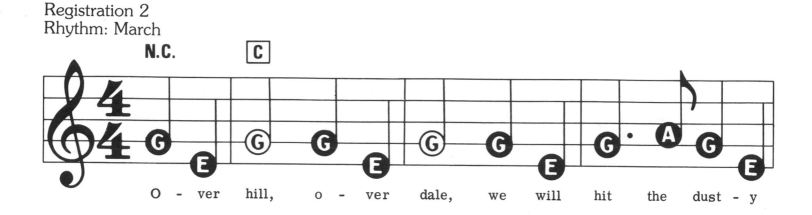

O - ver hill, o - ver dale, we will hit the dust - y

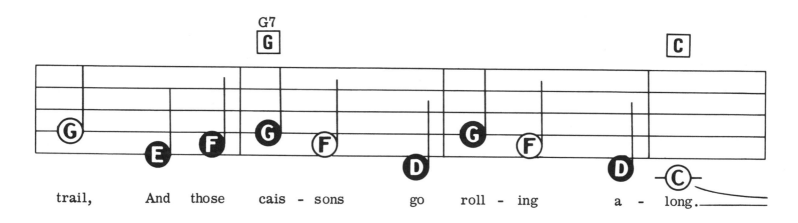

trail, And those cais - sons go roll - ing a - long.

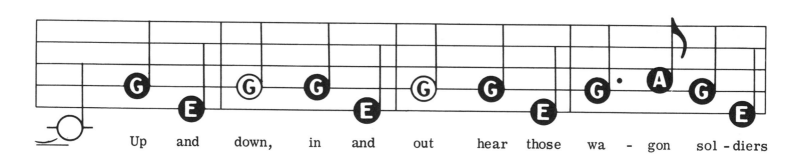

Up and down, in and out hear those wa - gon sol - diers

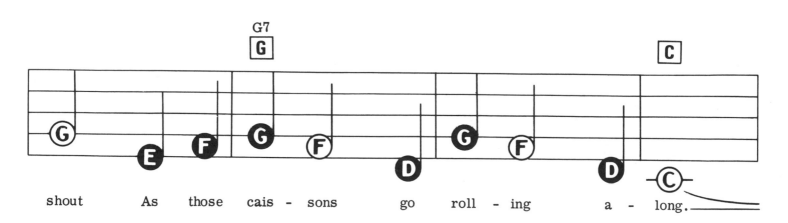

shout As those cais - sons go roll - ing a - long.

17

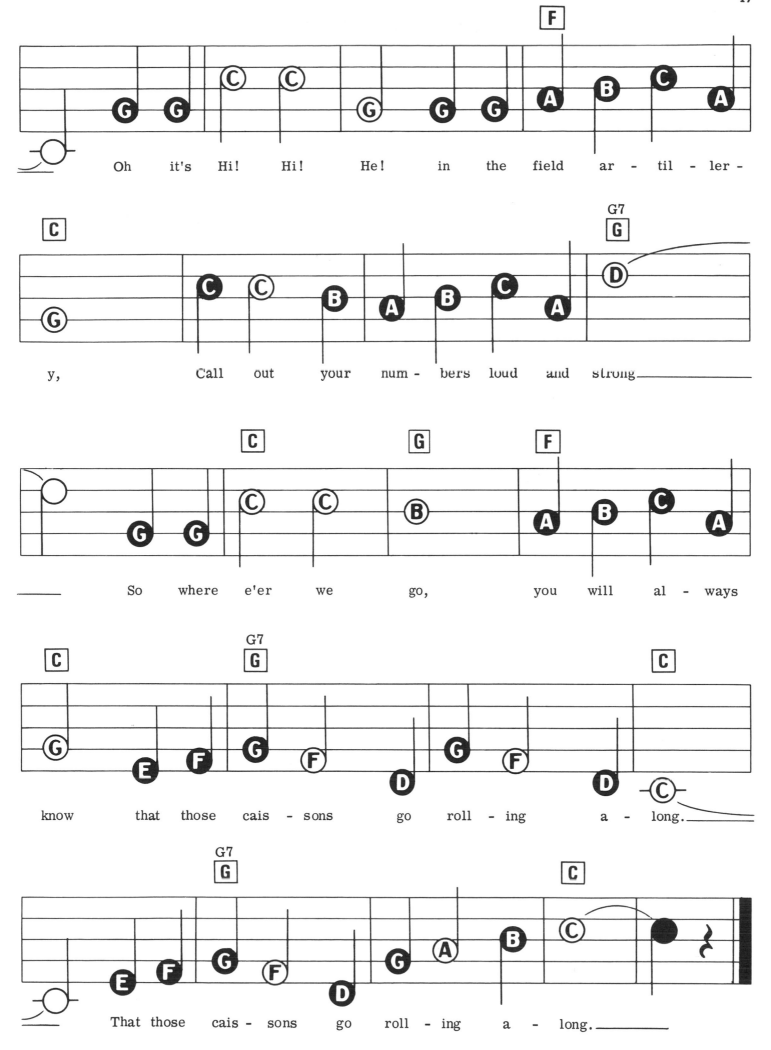

Can Can Polka

Registration 5
Rhythm: Polka or March

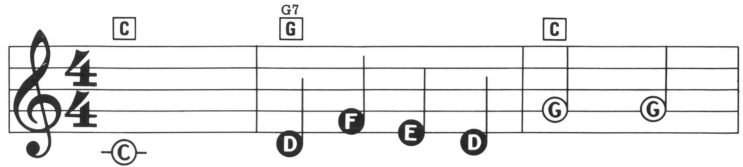

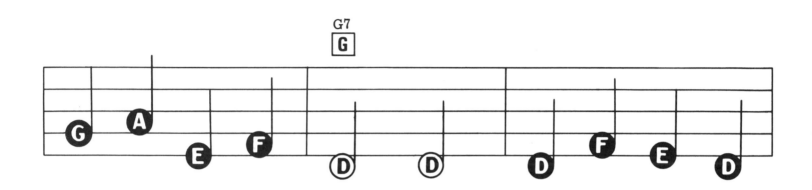

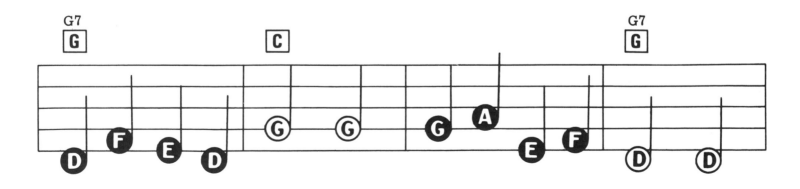

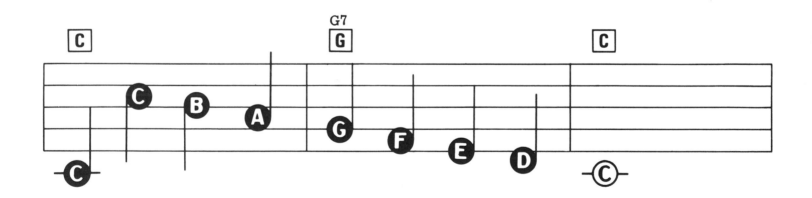

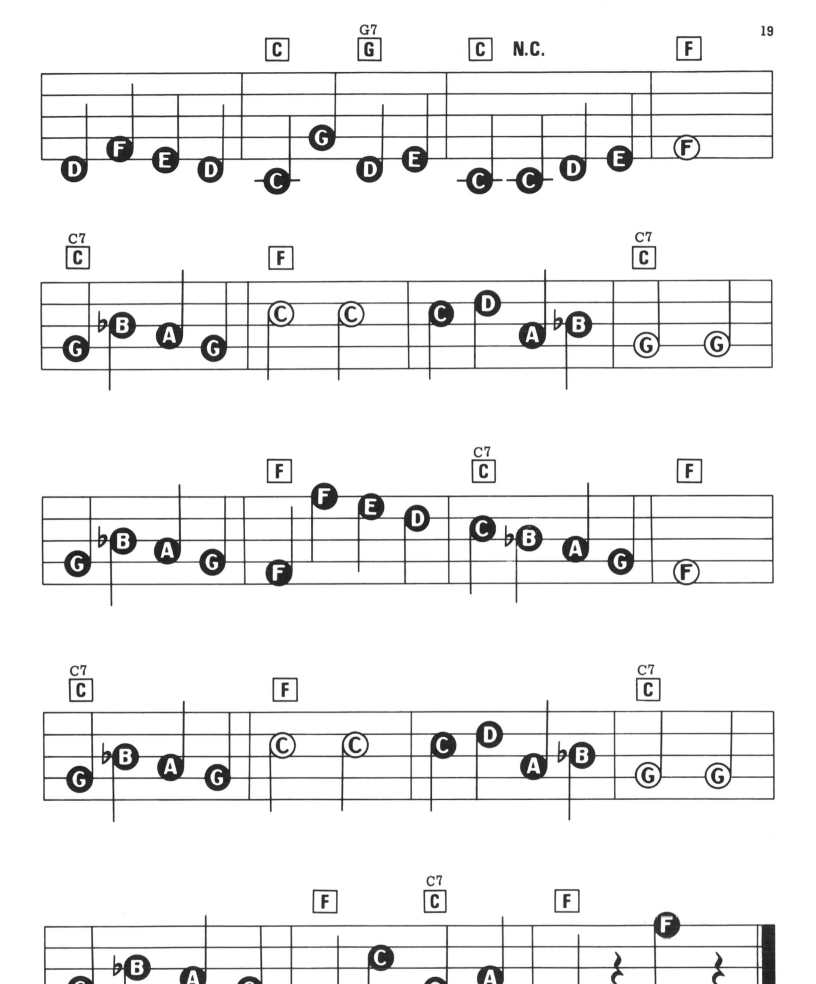

Chiapanecas

Registration 4
Rhythm: Waltz

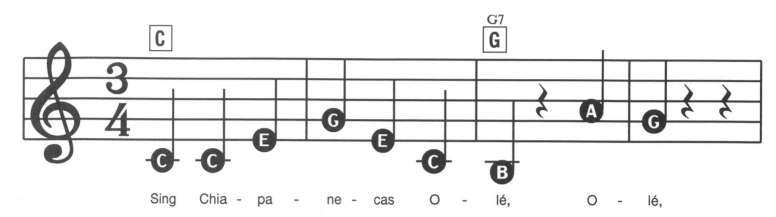

Sing Chia - pa - ne - cas O - lé, O - lé,

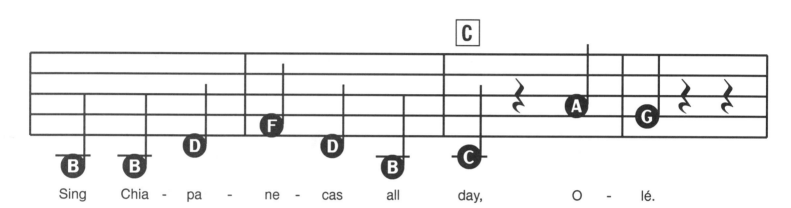

Sing Chia - pa - ne - cas all day, O - lé.

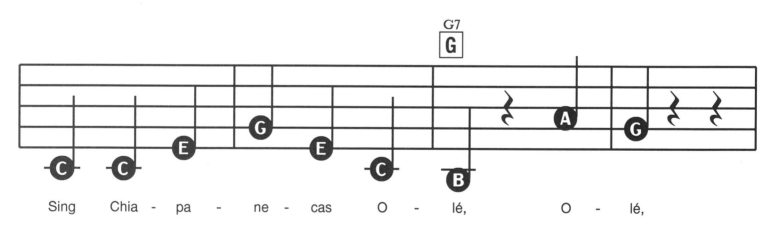

Sing Chia - pa - ne - cas O - lé, O - lé,

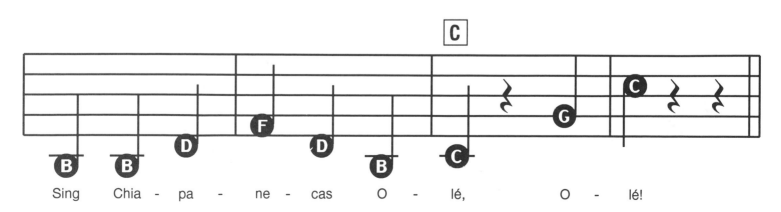

Sing Chia - pa - ne - cas O - lé, O - lé!

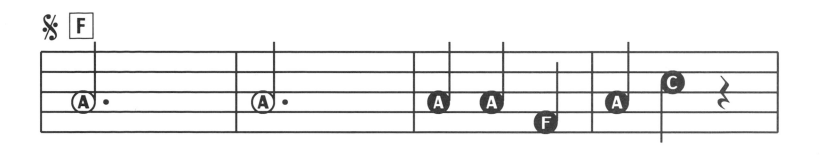

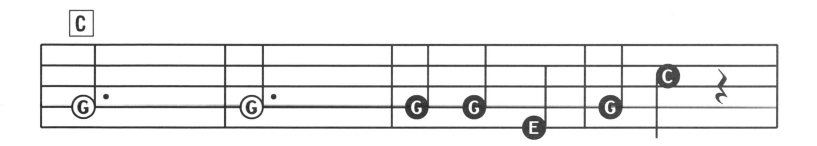

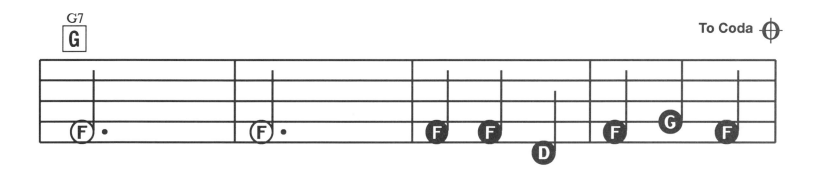

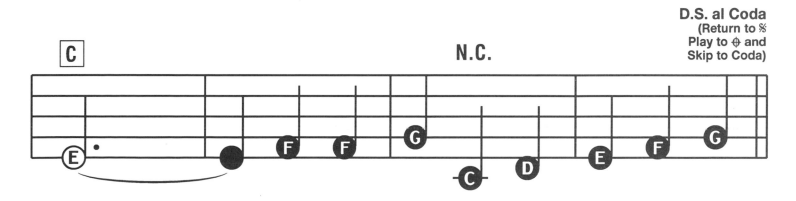

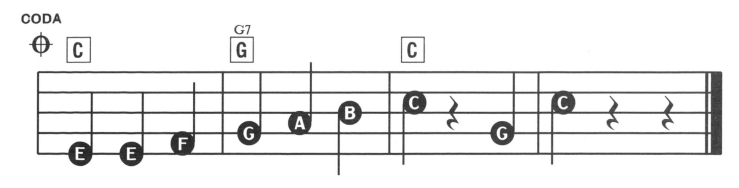

Cielito Lindo

Registration 4
Rhythm: Waltz

Mexican

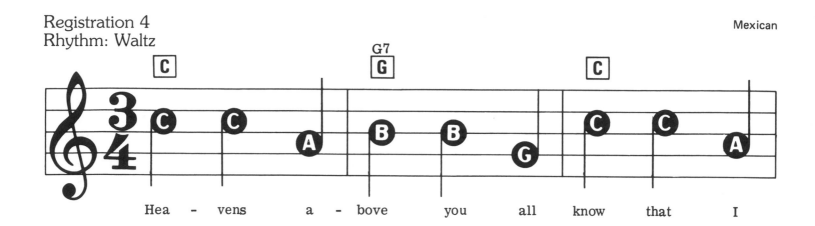

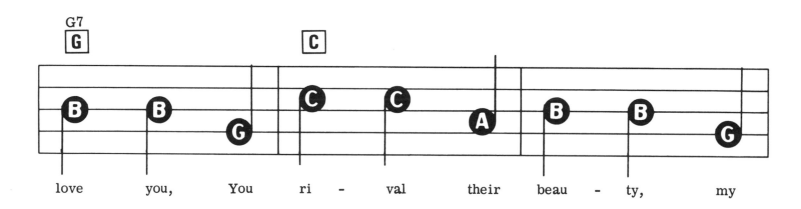

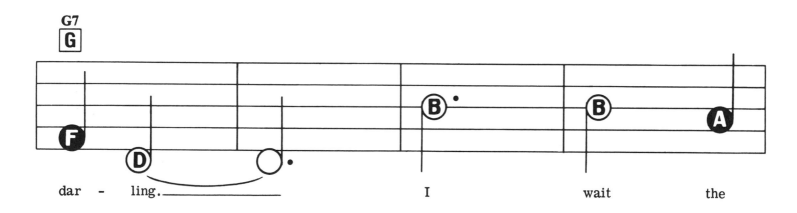

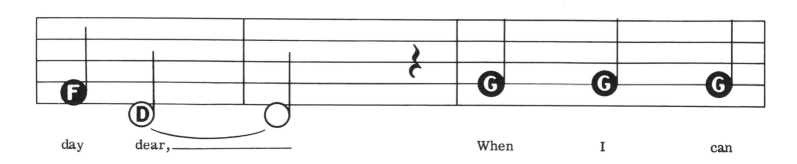

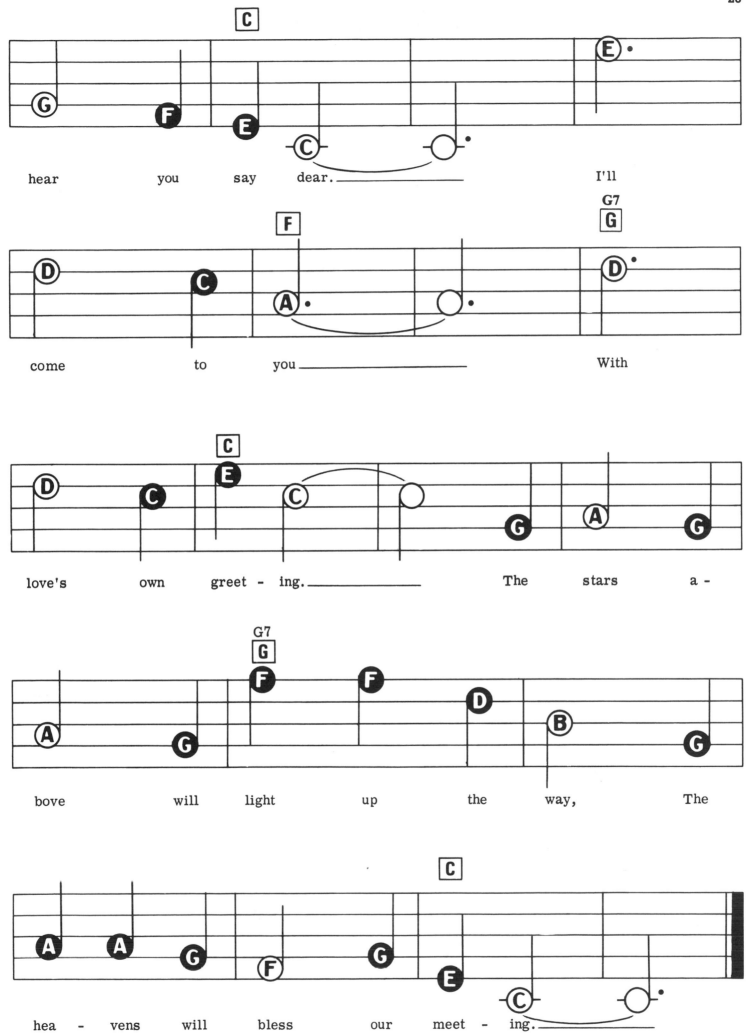

Clementine

Registration 2
Rhythm: Waltz

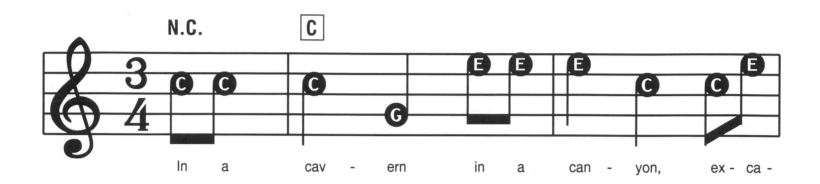

In a cav - ern in a can - yon, ex - ca -

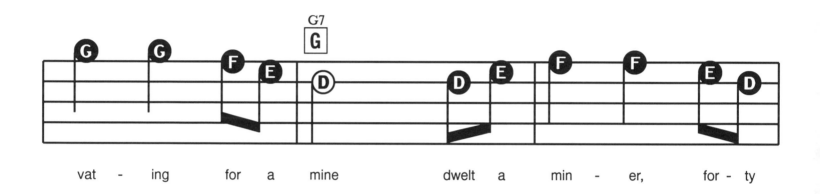

vat - ing for a mine dwelt a min - er, for - ty

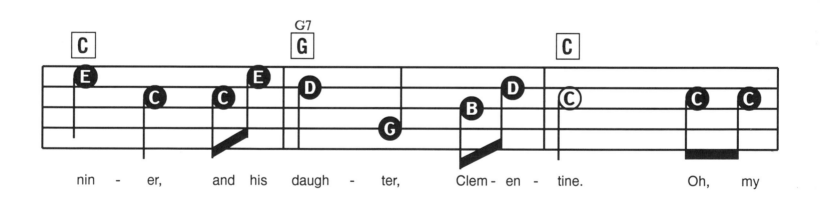

nin - er, and his daugh - ter, Clem - en - tine. Oh, my

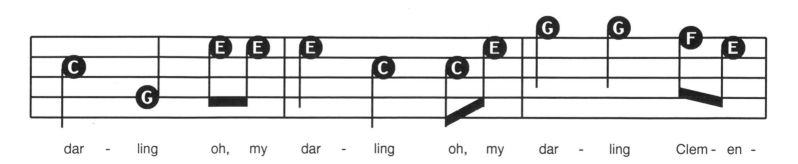

dar - ling oh, my dar - ling oh, my dar - ling Clem - en -

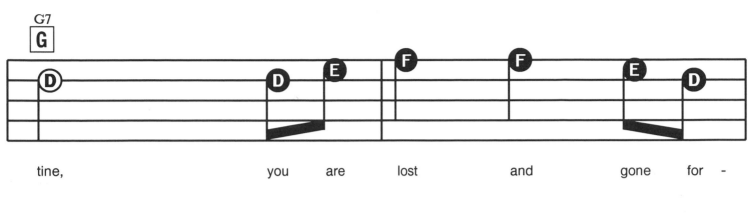

tine, you are lost and gone for -

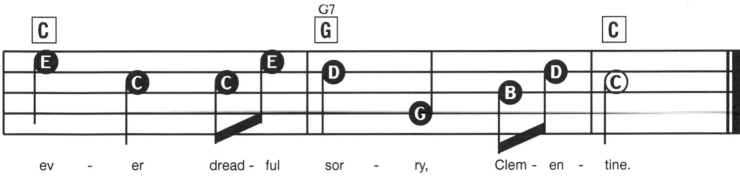

ev - er dread - ful sor - ry, Clem - en - tine.

Additional Lyrics

2. Light she was and, like a fairy,
   And her shoes were number nine,
   Herring boxes, without topses,
   Sandals were for Clementine.
   Chorus

3. Drove she ducklings to the water,
   Every morning just at nine,
   Stubbed her toe upon a splinter,
   Fell into the foaming brine.
   Chorus

4. Ruby lips above the water
   Blowing bubbles soft and fine,
   But alas I was no swimmer,
   So I lost my Clementine.
   Chorus

5. There's a churchyard, on the hillside,
   Where the flowers grow and twine,
   There grow roses, 'mongst the posies,
   Fertilized by Clementine.
   Chorus

Drink To Me Only With Thine Eyes

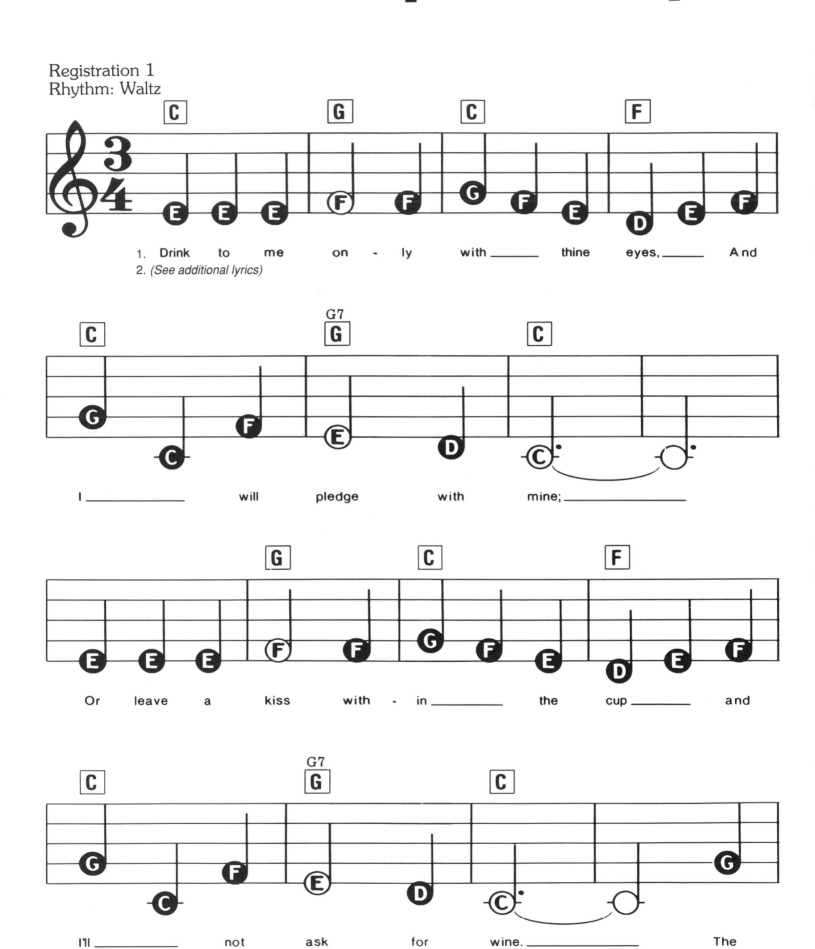

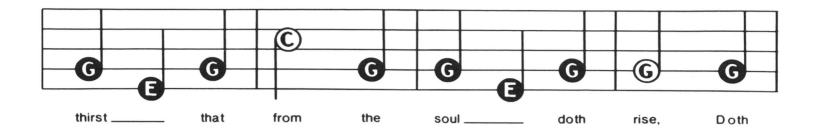

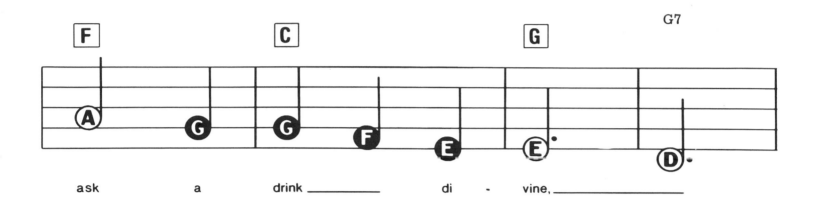

thirst _____ that from the soul _____ doth rise, Doth

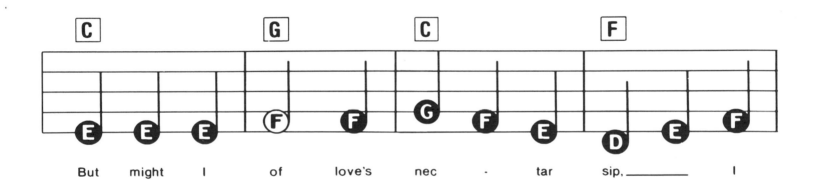

ask a drink _____ di - vine, _____

C   G   C   F

But might I of love's nec - tar sip, _____ I

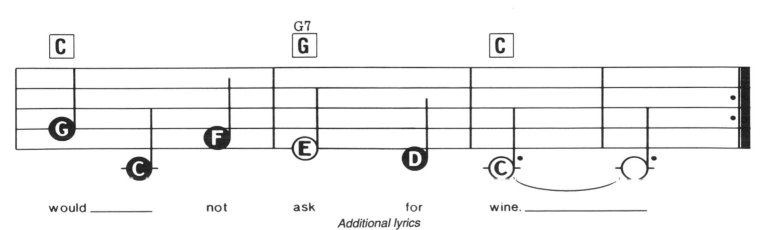

would _____ not ask for wine. _____

Additional lyrics

2. I sent thee late a rosy wreath,
Not so much honouring thee,
As giving it a hope that there
It could not withered be.
But thou thereon didst only breathe,
And send'st it back to me,
Since when it grows and smells, I swear,
Not of itself, but thee.

Du, Du Liegst Mir Im Herzen

Registration 4
Rhythm: Waltz

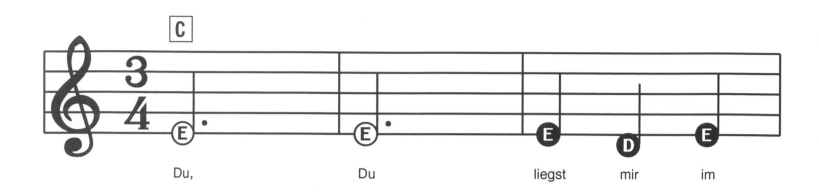

Du,   Du   liegst   mir   im

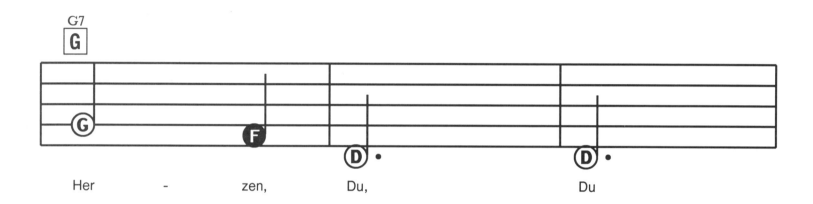

Her - zen,   Du,   Du

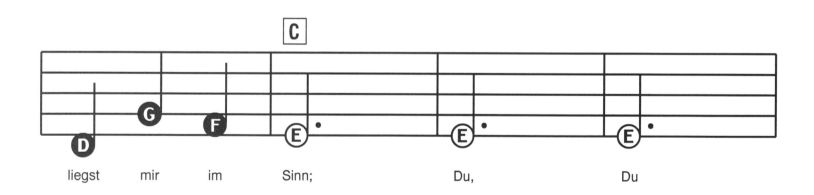

liegst mir   im   Sinn;   Du,   Du

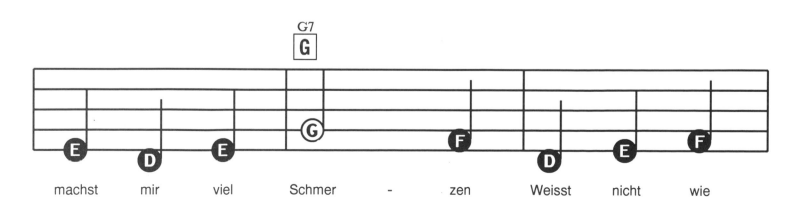

machst   mir   viel   Schmer - zen   Weisst   nicht   wie

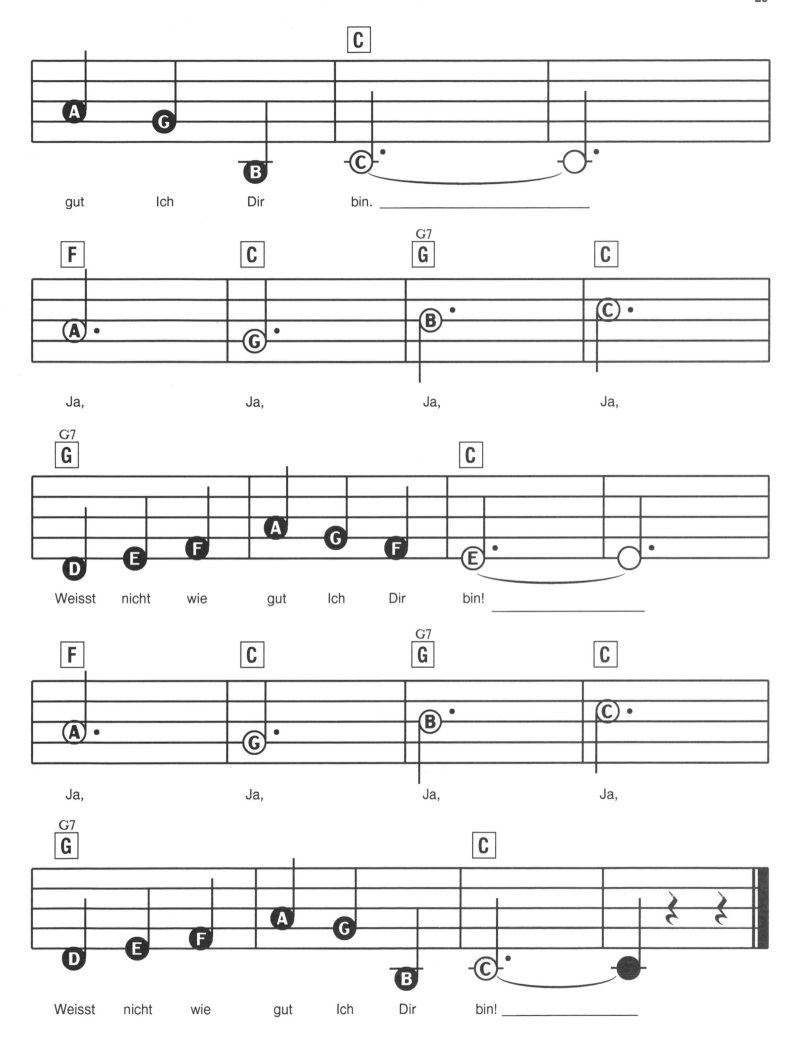

Fascination

Registration 10
Rhythm: Waltz

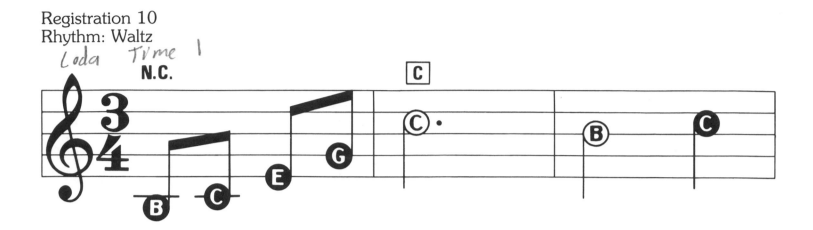

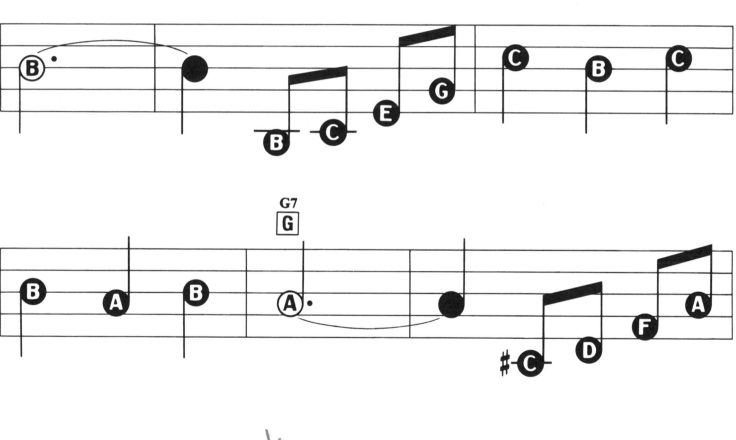

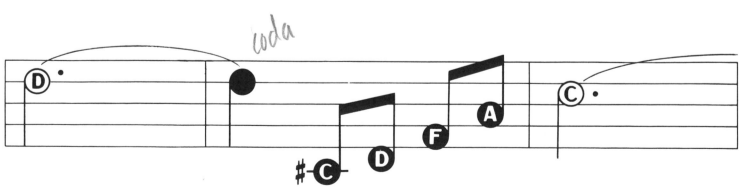

For He's A Jolly Good Fellow

Registration 4
Rhythm: Waltz

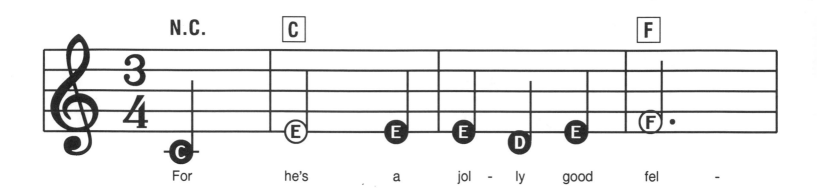

For he's a jol - ly good fel -

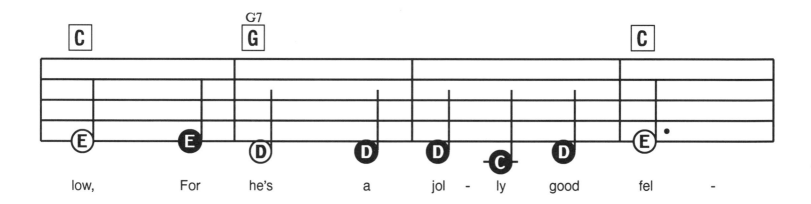

low, For he's a jol - ly good fel -

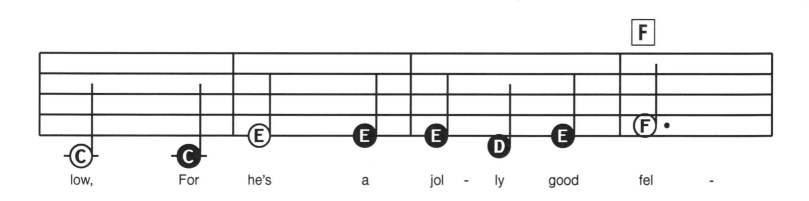

low, For he's a jol - ly good fel -

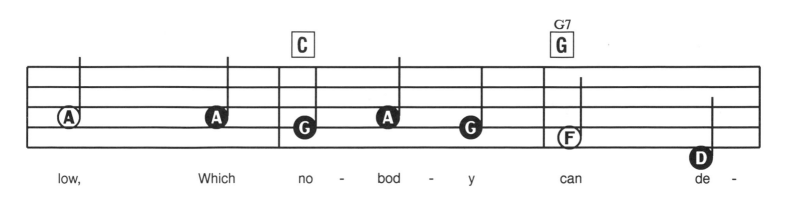

low, Which no - bod - y can de -

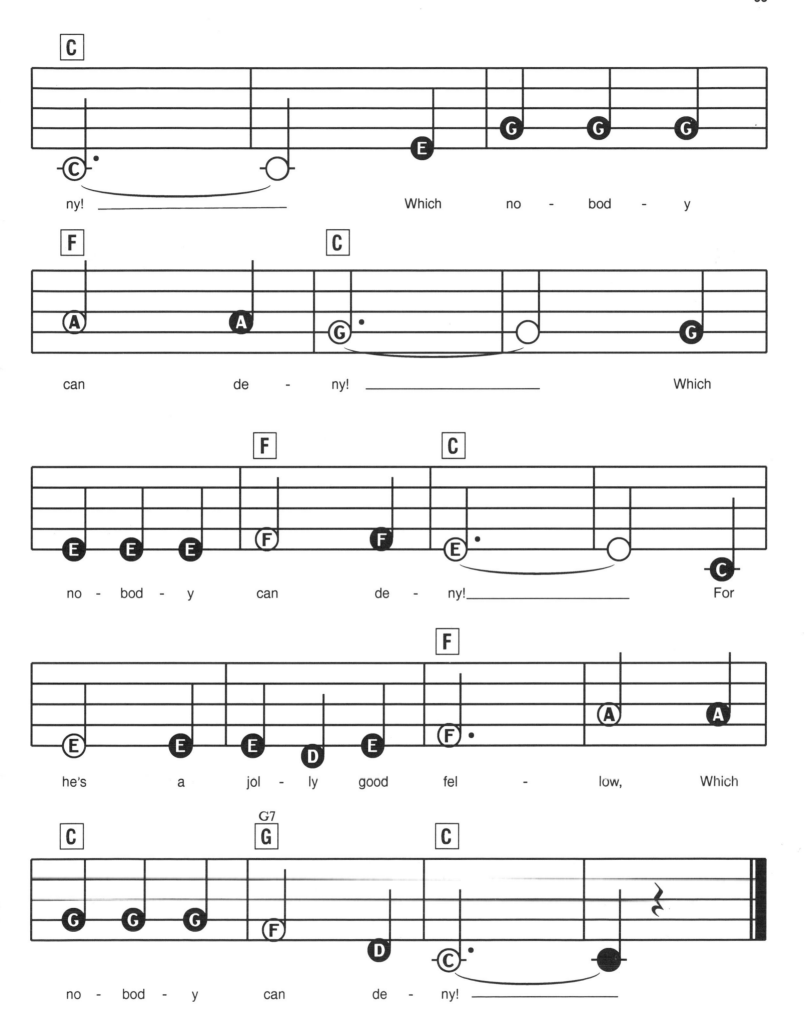

Frankie And Johnny

Registration 4
Rhythm: Swing

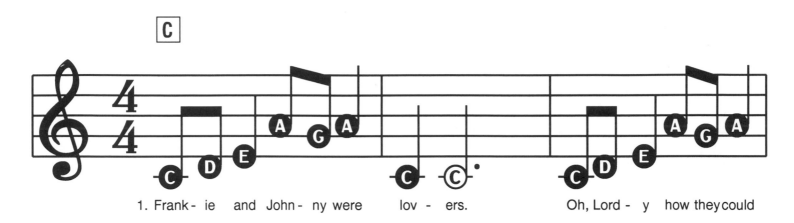

1. Frank-ie and John-ny were lov-ers. Oh, Lord-y how they could

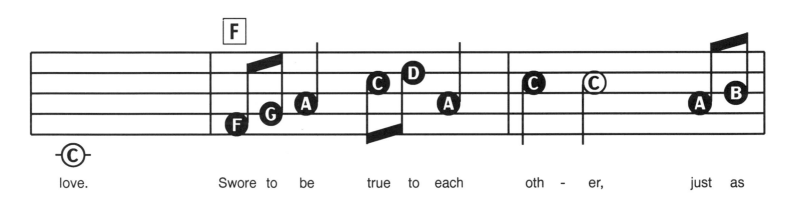

love. Swore to be true to each oth-er, just as

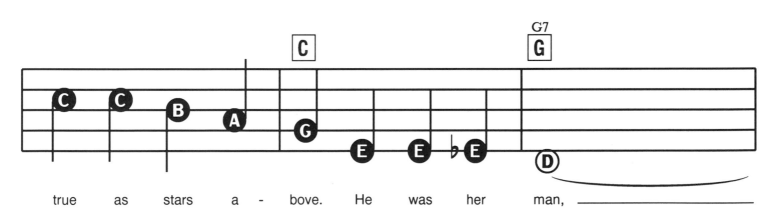

true as stars a-bove. He was her man,

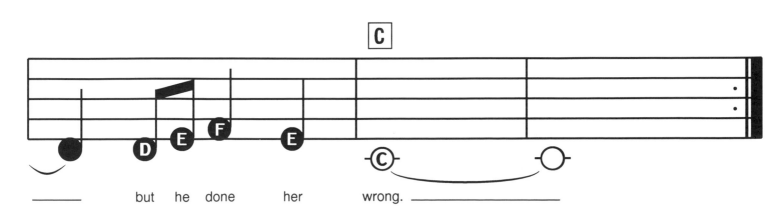

but he done her wrong.

Additional Lyrics

2. Frankie she was a good woman
   As everybody know,
   Spent a hundred dollars
   Just to buy her man some clothes.
   He was her man, but he was doing her wrong.

3. Frankie went down to the corner
   Just for a bucket of beer,
   Said: "Mr. bartender
   Has my loving Johnny been here?
   "He was my man, but he's a-doing me wrong."

4. "Now I don't want to tell you no stories
   And I don't want to tell you no lies
   I saw your man about an hour ago
   With a gal named Nellie Bligh
   He was your man, but he's a-doing you wrong."

5. Frankie she went down to the hotel
   Didn't go there for fun,
   Underneath her kimono
   She carried a forty-four gun.
   He was her man, but he was doing her wrong.

6. Frankie looked over the transom
   To see what she could spy,
   There sat Johnny on the sofa
   Just loving up Nellie Bligh.
   He was her man, but he was doing her wrong.

7. Frankie got down from that high stool
   She didn't want to see no more;
   Rooty-toot-toot three times she shot
   Right through that hardwood door.
   He was her man, but he was doing her wrong.

8. Now the first time that Frankie shot Johnny
   He let out an awful yell,
   Second time she shot him
   There was a new man's face in hell.
   He was her man, but he was doing her wrong.

9. "Oh roll me over easy
   Roll me over slow
   Roll me over on the right side
   For the left side hurts me so."
   He was her man, but he was doing her wrong.

10. Sixteen rubber-tired carriages
    Sixteen rubber-tired hacks
    They take poor Johnny to the graveyard
    They ain't gonna bring him back.
    He was her man, but he was doing her wrong.

11. Frankie looked out of the jailhouse
    To see what she could see,
    All she could hear was a two-string bow
    Crying nearer my God to thee.
    He was her man, but he was doing her wrong.

12. Frankie she said to the sheriff
    "What do you reckon they'll do?"
    Sheriff he said "Frankie,
    "It's the electric chair for you."
    He was her man, but he was doing her wrong.

13. This story has no moral
    This story has no end
    This story only goes to show
    That there ain't no good in men!
    He was her man, but he was doing her wrong.

He's Got The Whole World In His Hands

Registration 6
Rhythm: Swing or Rock

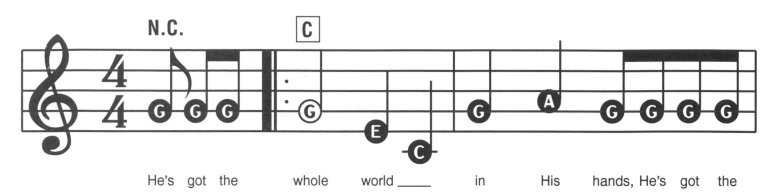

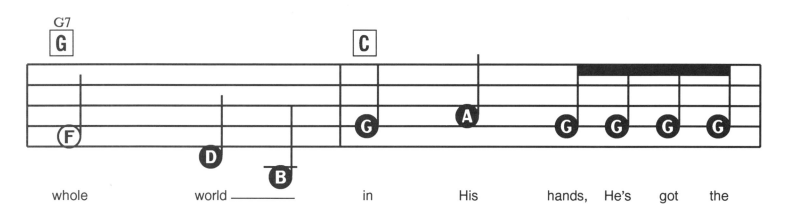

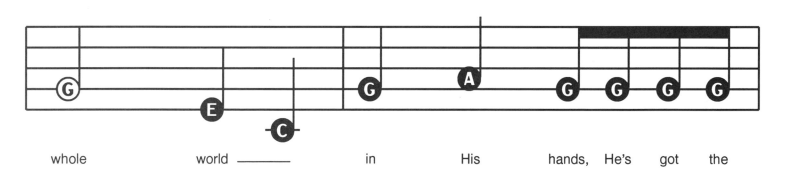

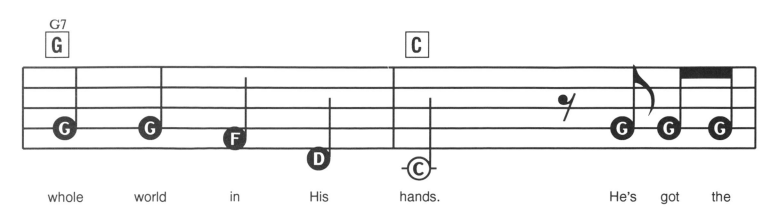

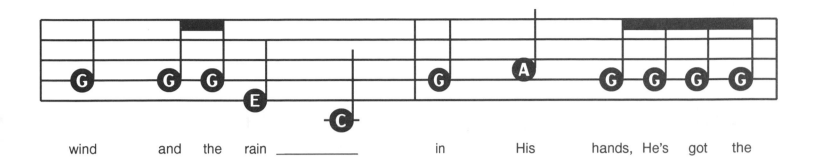

wind   and   the   rain _____   in   His   hands, He's   got   the

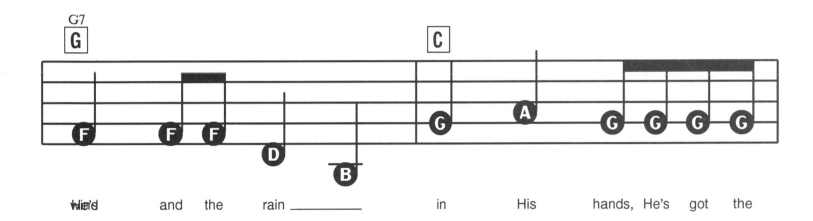

wind   and   the   rain _____   in   His   hands, He's   got   the

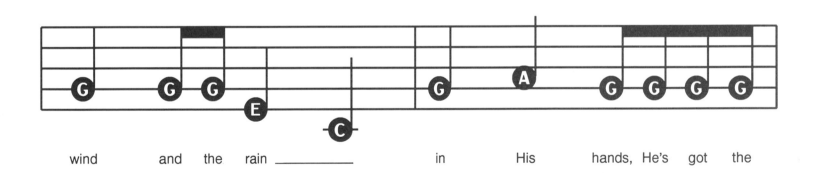

wind   and   the   rain _____   in   His   hands, He's   got   the

Repeat and Fade

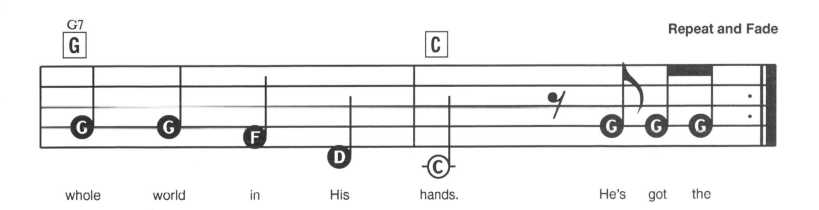

whole   world   in   His   hands.   He's   got   the

Home Sweet Home

Registration 9
Rhythm: Ballad or Pops

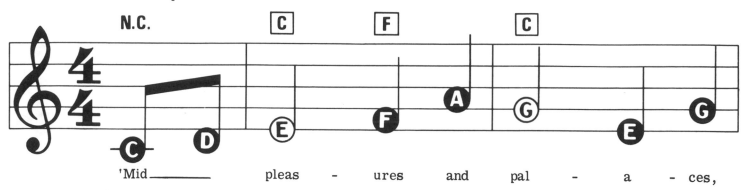

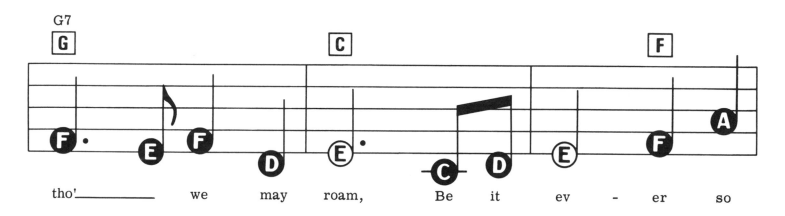

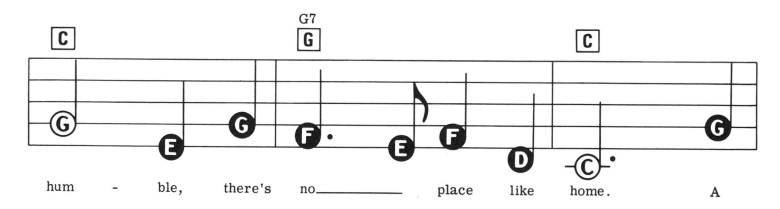

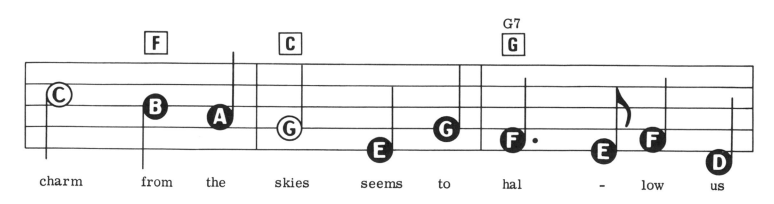

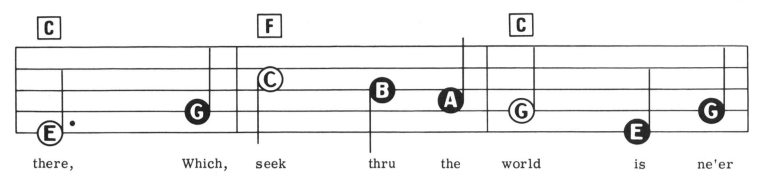

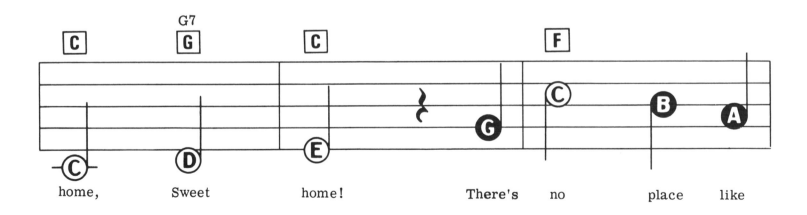

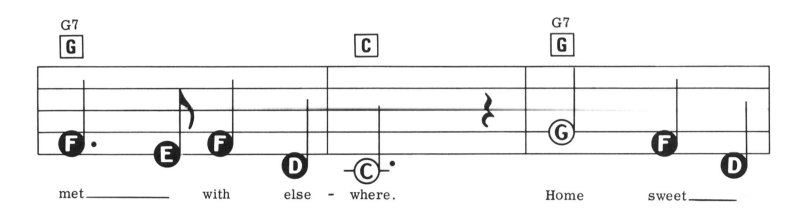

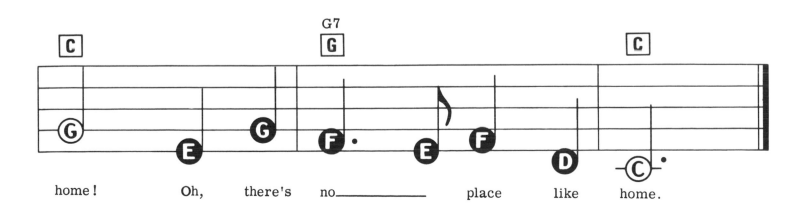

Just A Closer Walk With Thee

Registration 2
Rhythm: Swing

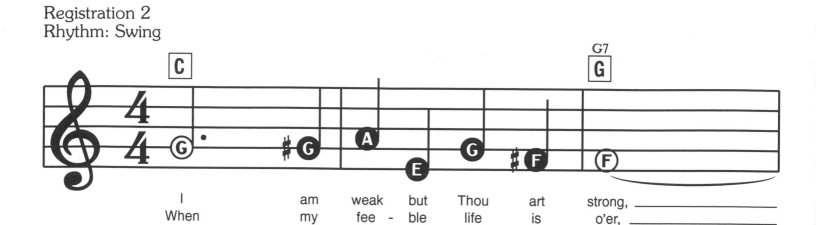

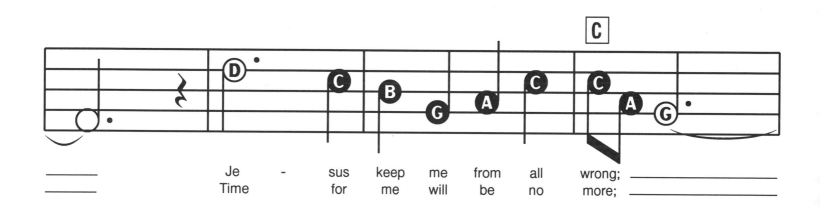

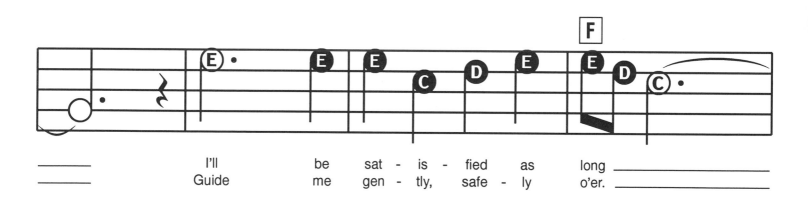

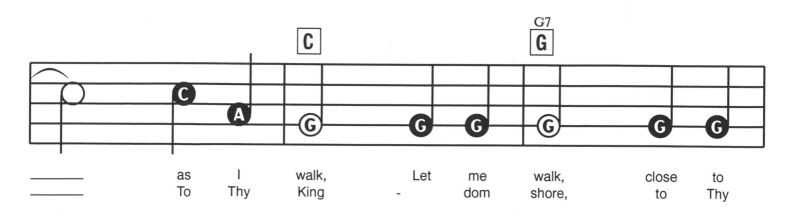

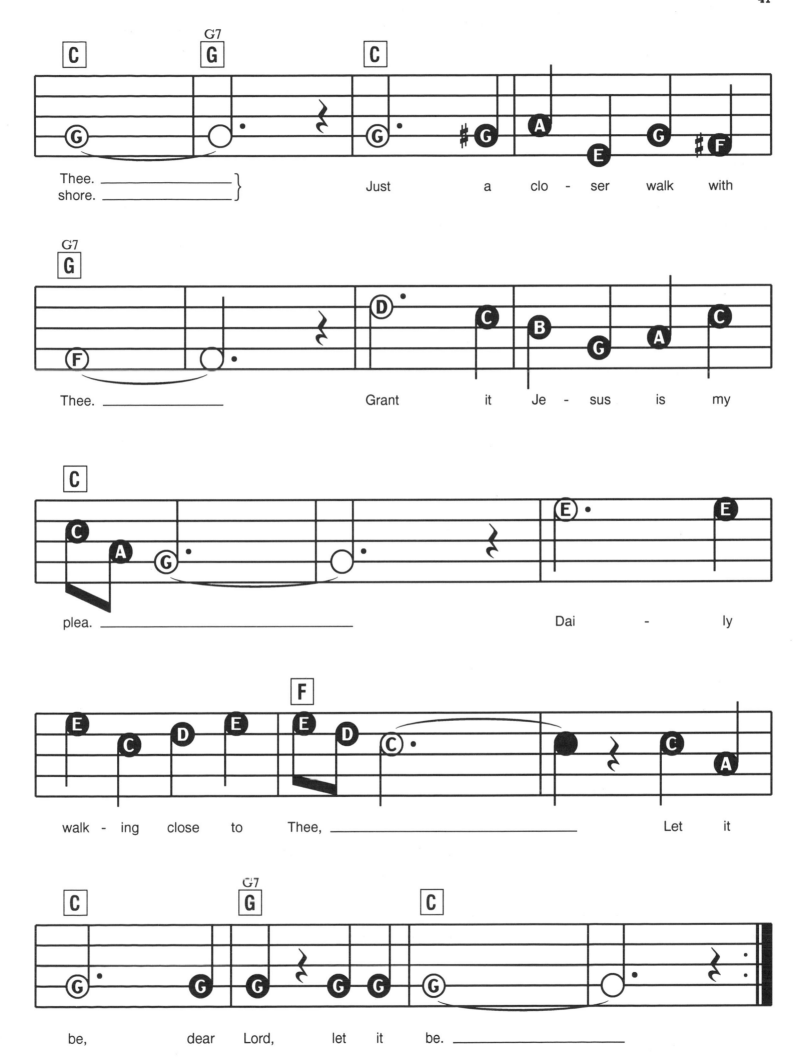

Kumbaya

Registration 3
Rhythm: 8 Beat or Rock

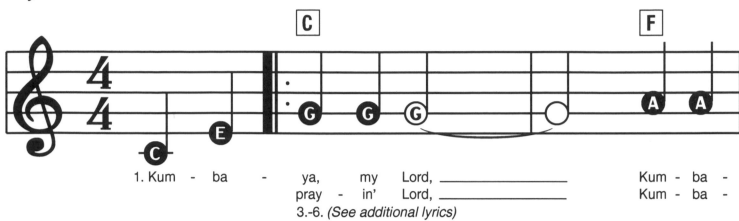

1. Kum - ba - ya, my Lord, _____ Kum - ba -
   pray - in' Lord, _____ Kum - ba -
3.-6. *(See additional lyrics)*

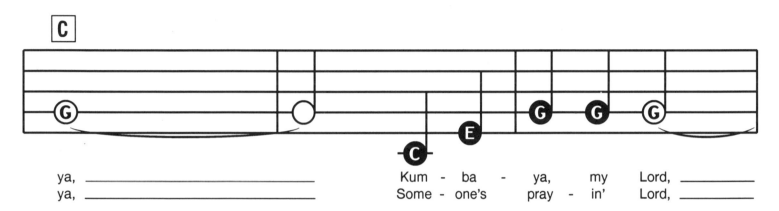

ya, _____ Kum - ba - ya, my Lord, _____
ya, _____ Some - one's pray - in' Lord, _____

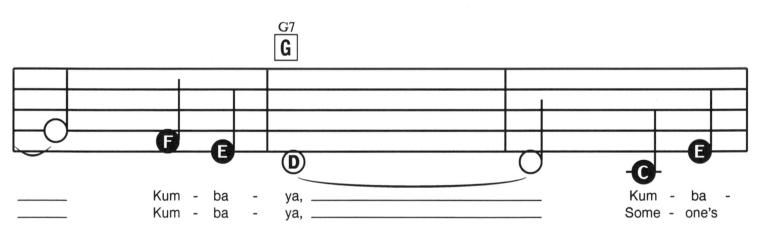

_____ Kum - ba - ya, _____ Kum - ba -
_____ Kum - ba - ya, _____ Some - one's

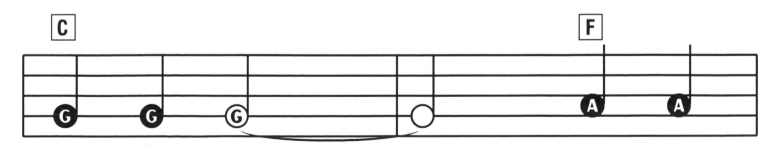

ya, my Lord, _____ Kum - ba -
pray - in' Lord, _____ Kum - ba -

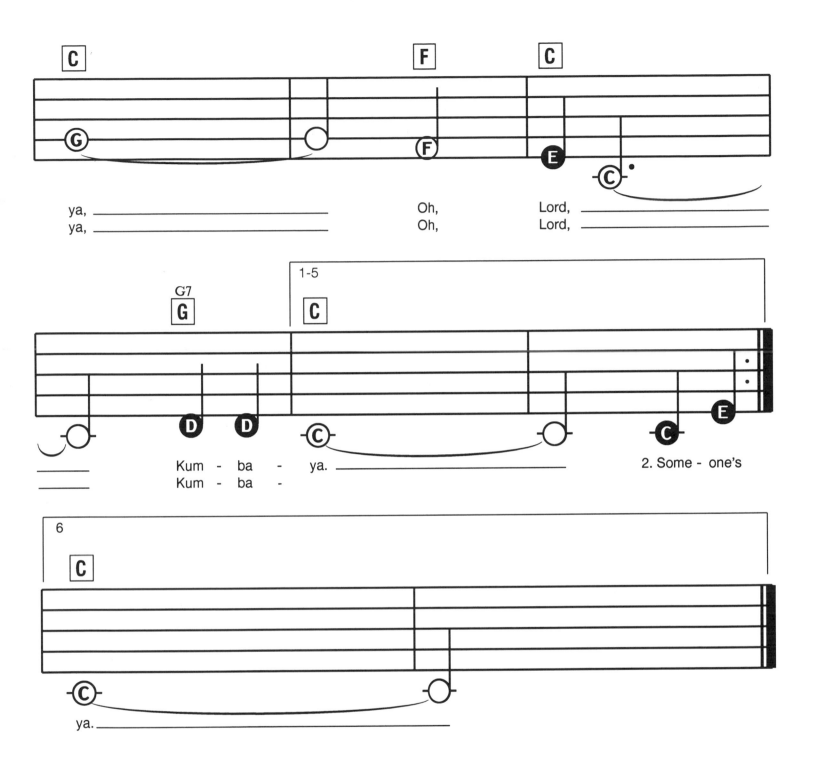

Additional Lyrics

3. Someone's singin', Lord, Kum-bah-ya...
4. Someone's cryin', Lord, Kum-bah-ya...
5. Someone's dancin', Lord, Kum-bah-ya...
6 Someone's shoutin', Lord, Kum-bah-ya...

Londonderry Air

Registration 10
Rhythm: Ballad or none

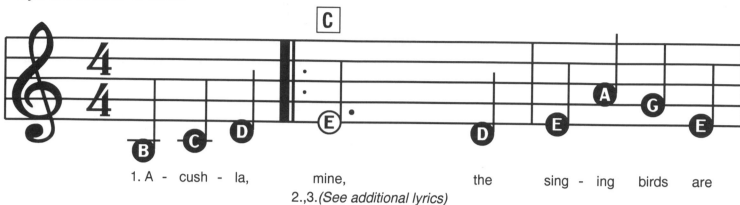

1. A - cush - la,   mine,   the   sing - ing   birds   are

2.,3.*(See additional lyrics)*

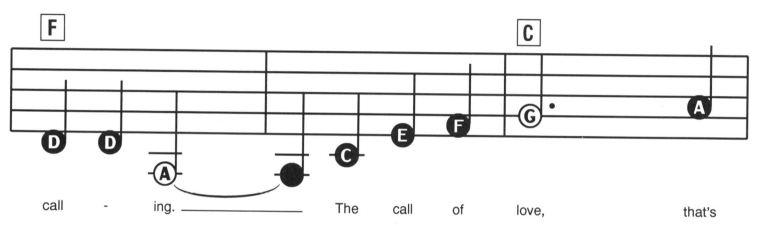

call - ing. _____ The   call   of   love,   that's

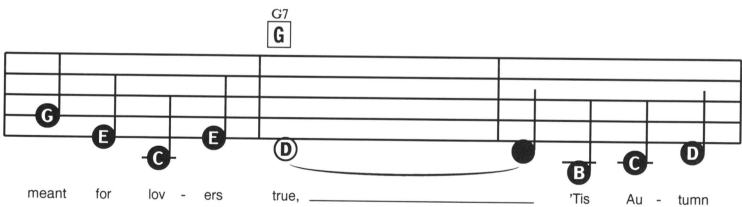

meant   for   lov - ers   true, _____ 'Tis   Au - tumn

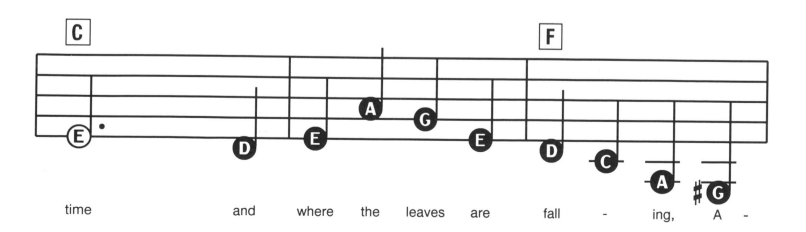

time   and   where   the   leaves   are   fall - ing,   A -

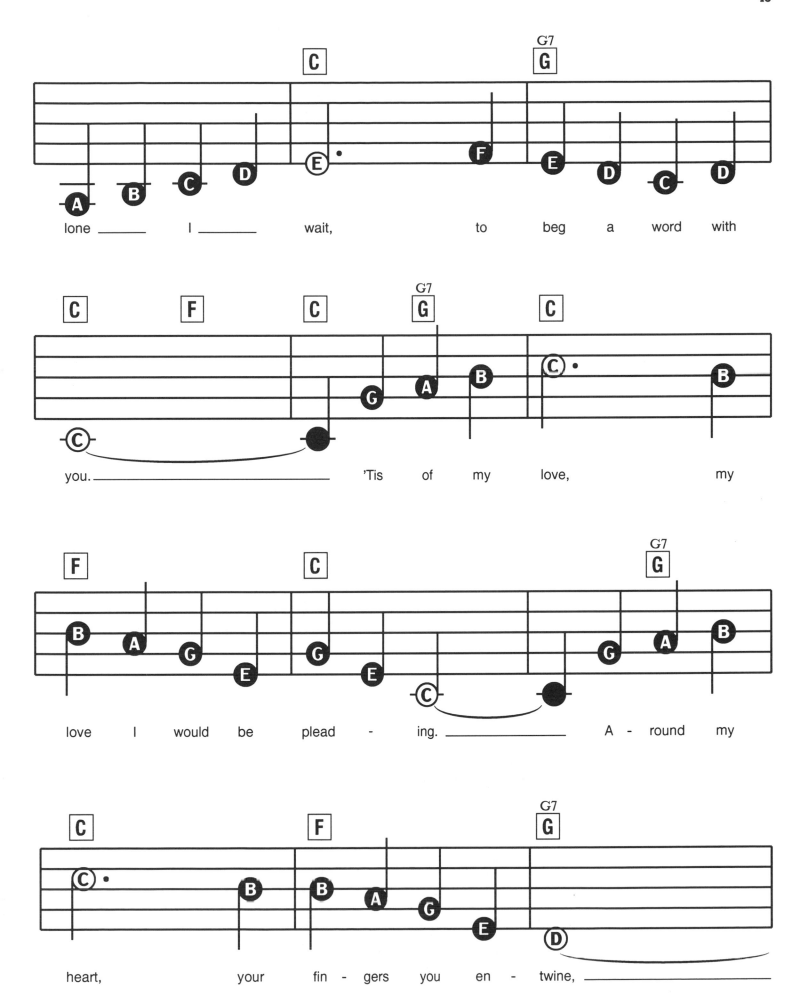

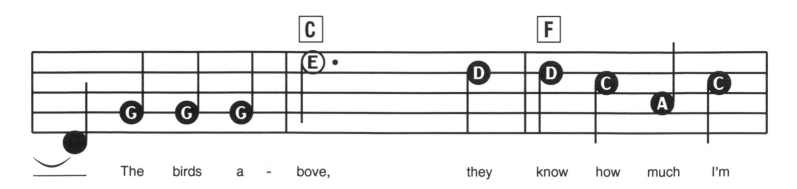

The birds a - bove, they know how much I'm

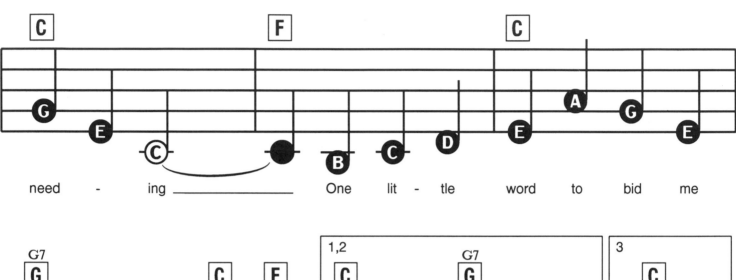

need - ing _____ One lit - tle word to bid me

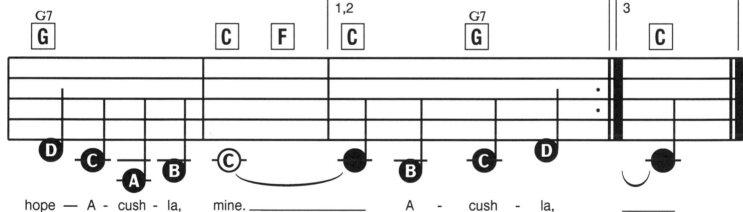

hope — A - cush - la, mine. _____ A - cush - la, _____

Additional Lyrics

2. Acushla, mine, your lips are ever smiling,
   They smiled their way into my longing heart,
   Your roguish eyes to me are so beguiling,
   I pray the Saints, that never we may part.
   When Winter comes, and all the world is dreary,
   And sun and stars no longer seem to shine,
   The world is dark, and I am sad and weary,
   'Tis then I need you most of all — Acushla, mine.

3. Acushla, mine, when birds again are singing,
   Their mating song, and all the land is gay,
   When, at the church, the wedding bells are ringing,
   Mavourneen, dear, 'twill be a happy day.
   And through the years no matter what the weather,
   Around my heart, your love will still entwine,
   We'll wander on, as long as we're together,
   And wander In to Paradise — Acushla, mine.

Marianne

Registration 4
Rhythm: Samba or Latin

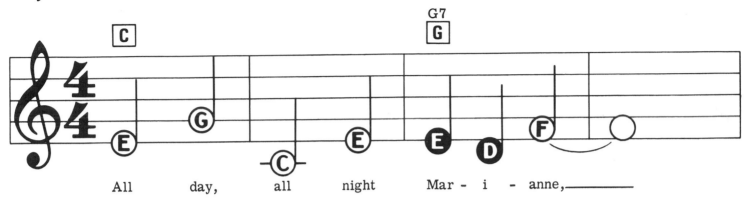

All day, all night Mar - i - anne,_____

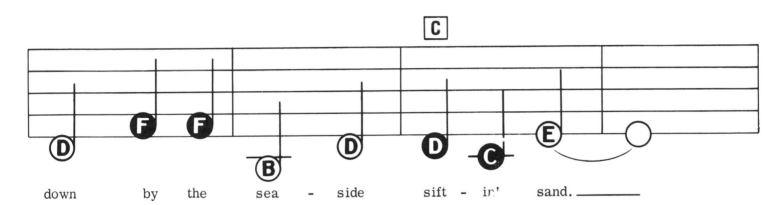

down by the sea - side sift - in' sand._____

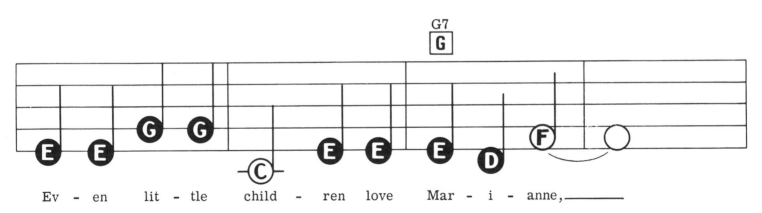

Ev - en lit - tle child - ren love Mar - i - anne,_____

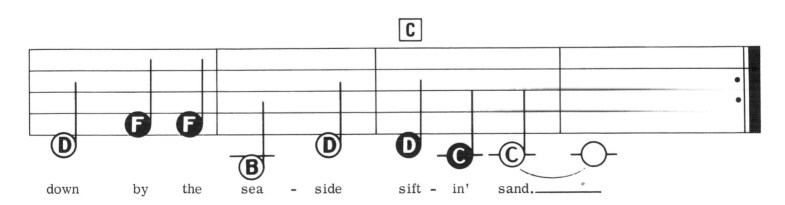

down by the sea - side sift - in' sand._____

Marine's Hymn

Registration 1
Rhythm: March

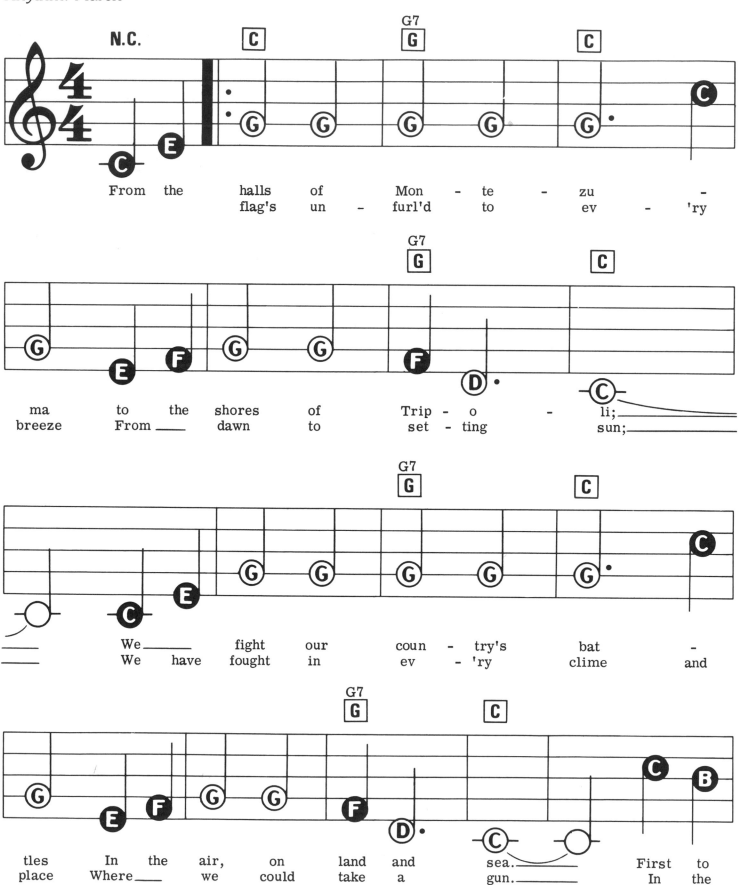

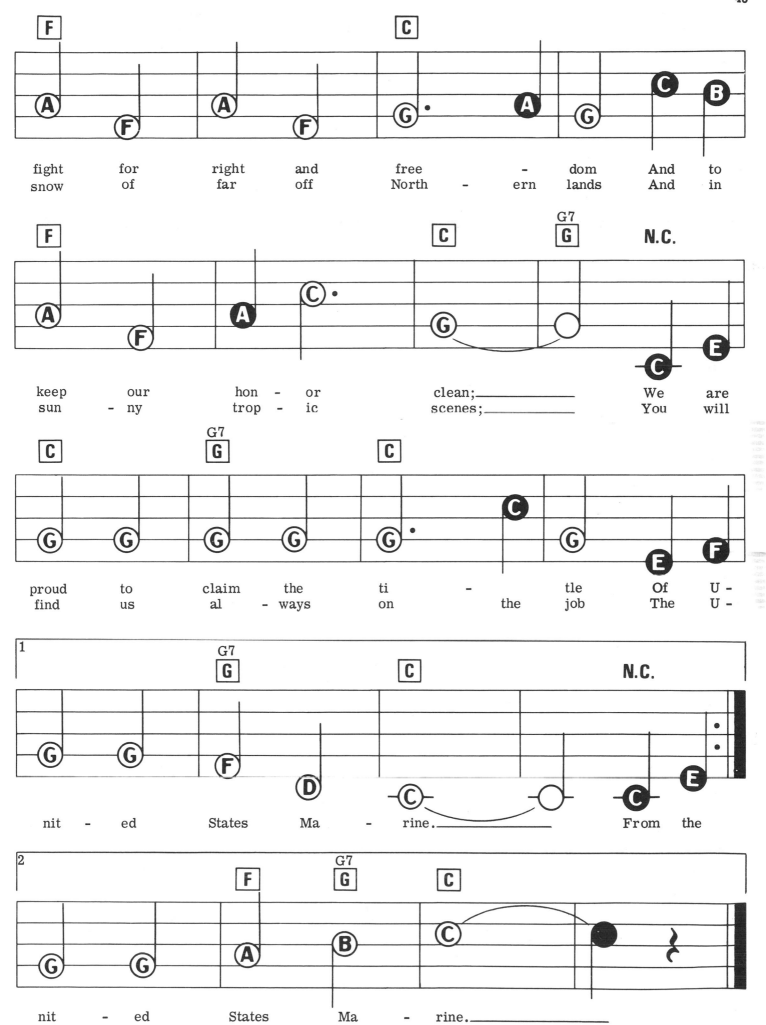

Michael, Row The Boat Ashore

Registration 2
Rhythm: Swing

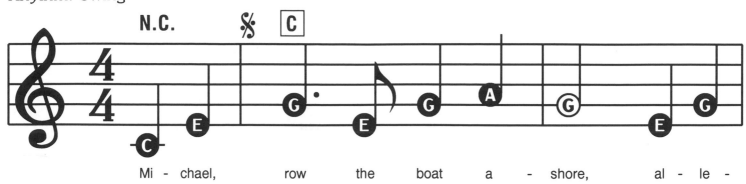

Mi - chael, row the boat a - shore, al - le -

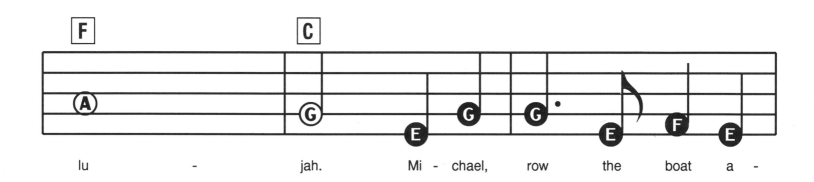

lu - jah. Mi - chael, row the boat a -

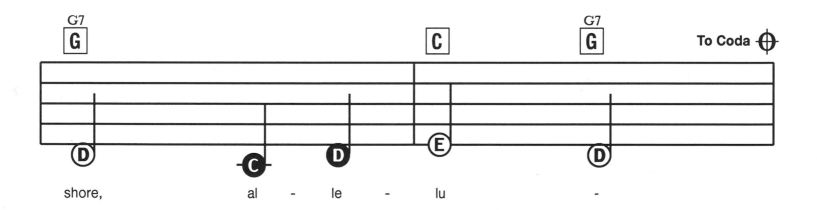

shore, al - le - lu -

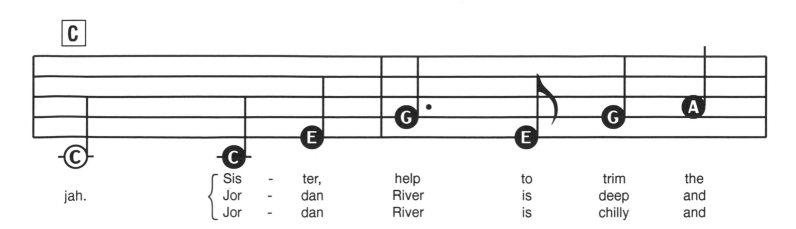

jah.

Sis - ter, help to trim the
Jor - dan River is deep and
Jor - dan River is chilly and

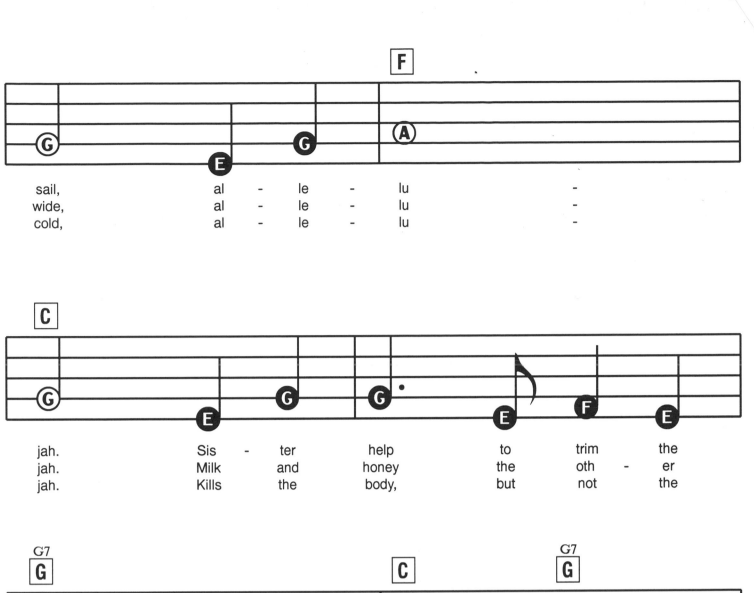

			sail,	al	–	le	–	lu	–
			wide,	al	–	le	–	lu	–
			cold,	al	–	le	–	lu	–

jah.		Sis	–	ter	help		to	trim	the
jah.		Milk	and	the	honey		the	oth	–	er
jah.		Kills	the	body,		but	not	the

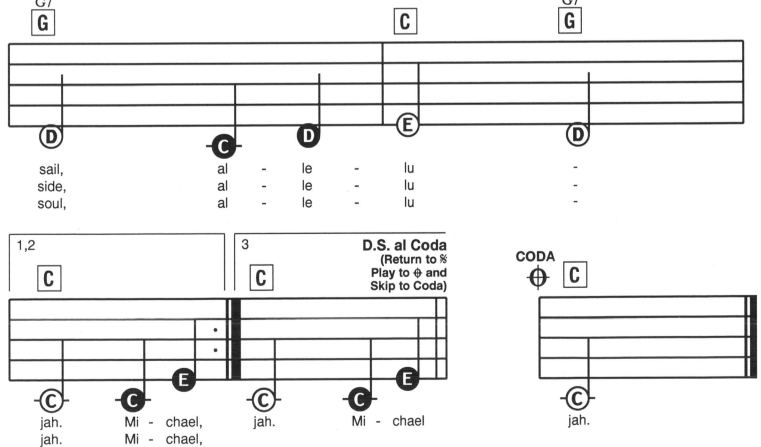

sail,	al	–	le	–	lu	–
side,	al	–	le	–	lu	–
soul,	al	–	le	–	lu	–

1,2

C

3   **D.S. al Coda**
(Return to %
Play to ⊕ and
Skip to Coda)

C

CODA

⊕ **C**

| jah. | | Mi | – | chael, | jah. | | Mi | – | chael | jah. |
| jah. | | Mi | – | chael, | | | | | | |

My Old Kentucky Home

Registration 5
Rhythm: Ballad

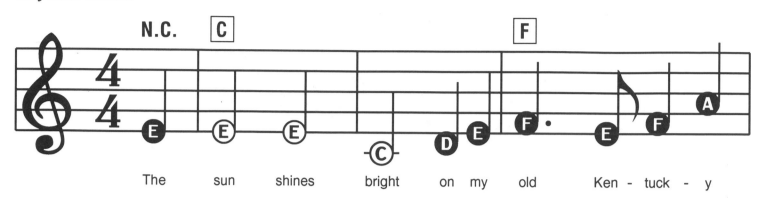

The sun shines bright on my old Ken - tuck - y

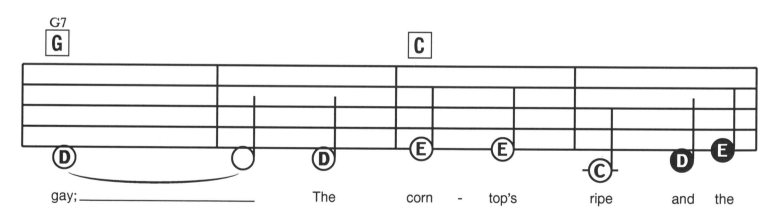

home, 'Tis sum - mer, the peo - ple are

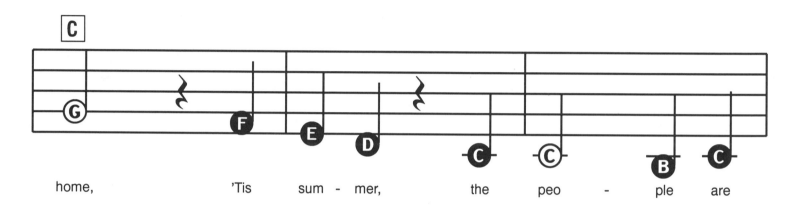

gay;_____ The corn - top's ripe and the

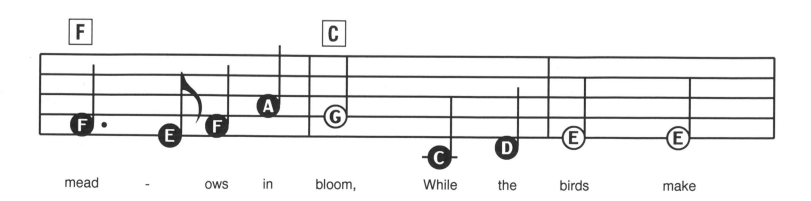

mead - ows in bloom, While the birds make

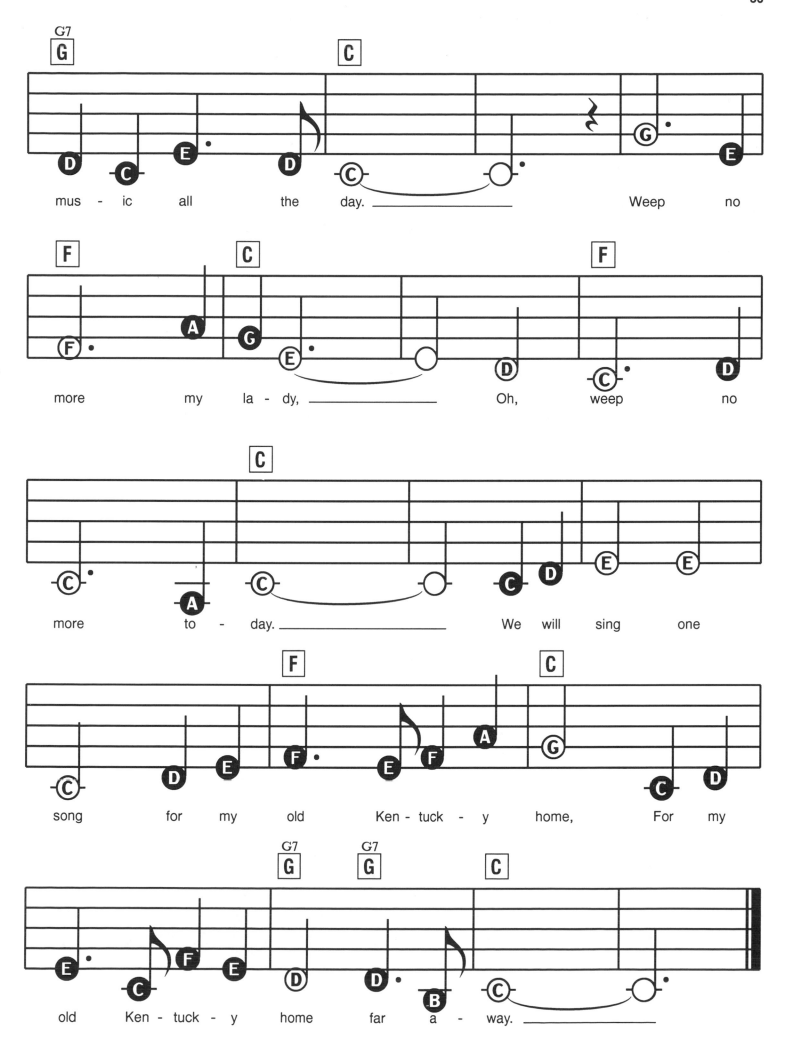

Ode To Joy

Registration 5
Rhythm: March

Music by Ludwig van Beethoven
Words adapted from Friedrich Schiller

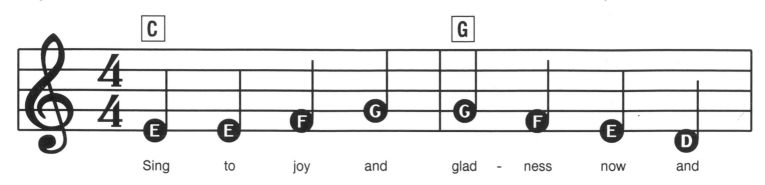

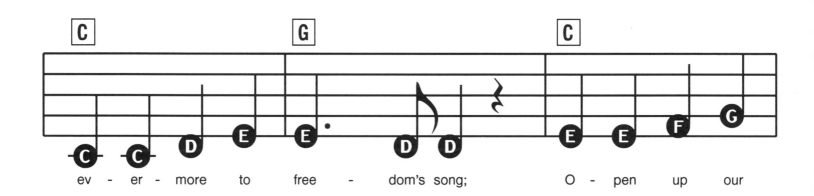

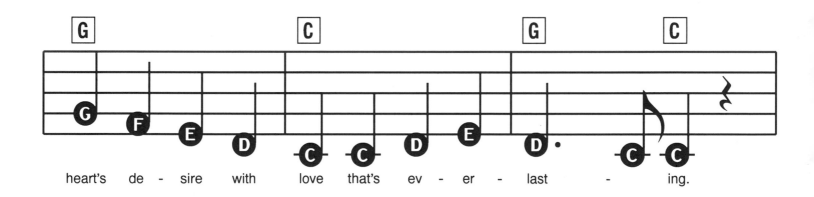

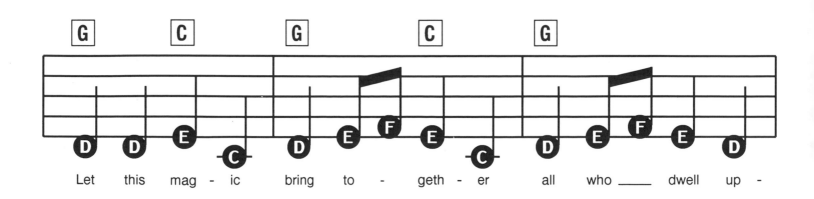

55

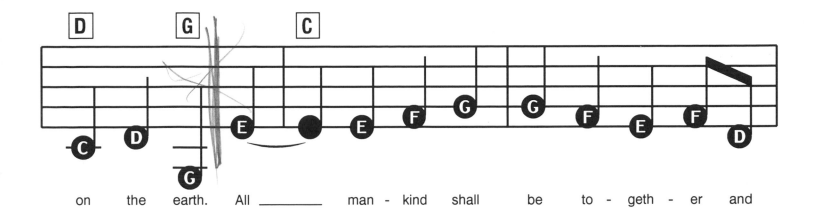

on the earth. All _____ man - kind shall be to - geth - er and

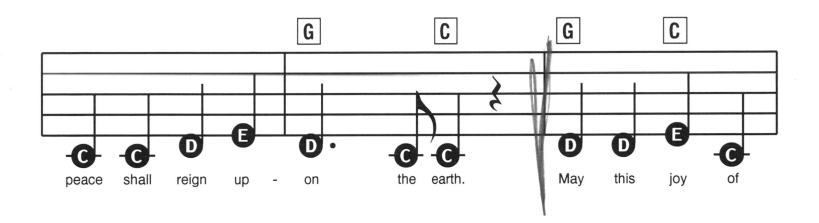

peace shall reign up - on the earth. May this joy of

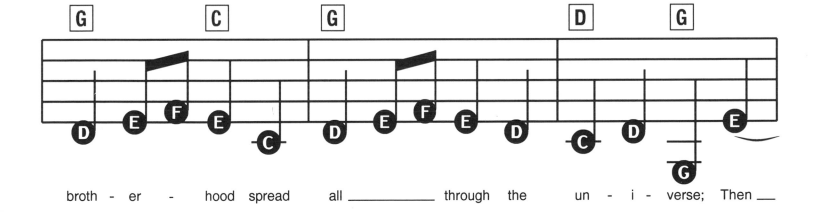

broth - er - hood spread all _____ through the un - i - verse; Then __

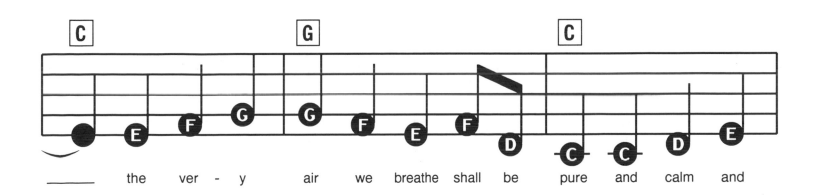

_____ the ver - y air we breathe shall be pure and calm and

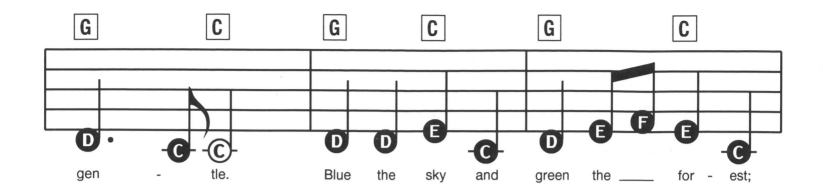

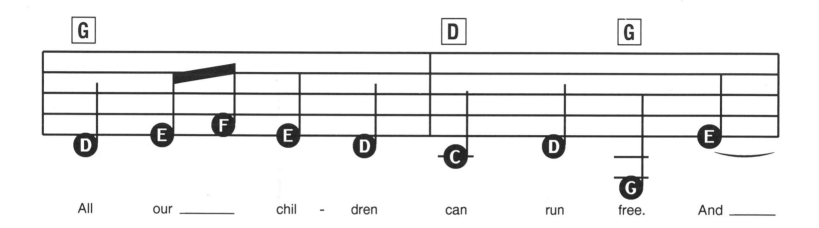

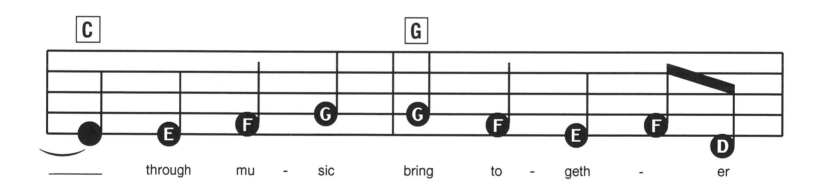

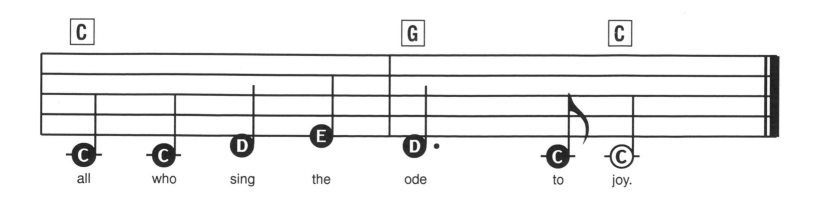

Oh! Susanna

Registration 3
Rhythm: Country

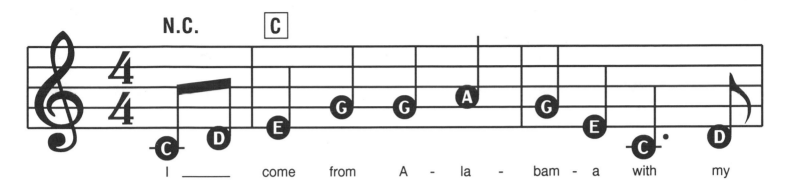

I _____ come from A - la - bam - a with my

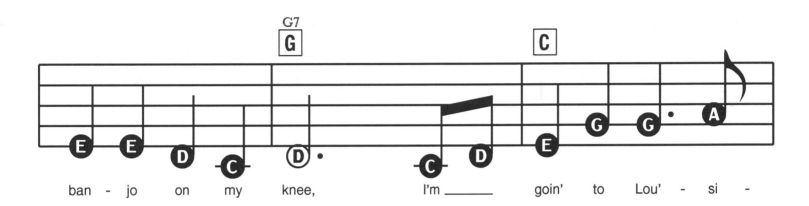

ban - jo on my knee, I'm _____ goin' to Lou' - si -

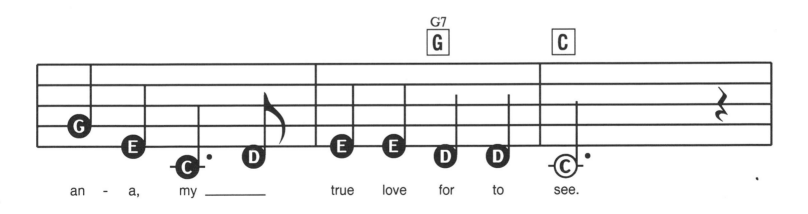

an - a, my _____ true love for to see.

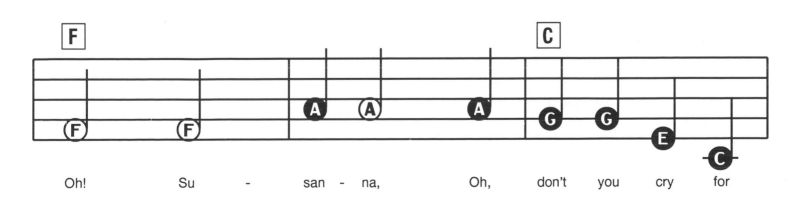

Oh! Su - san - na, Oh, don't you cry for

58

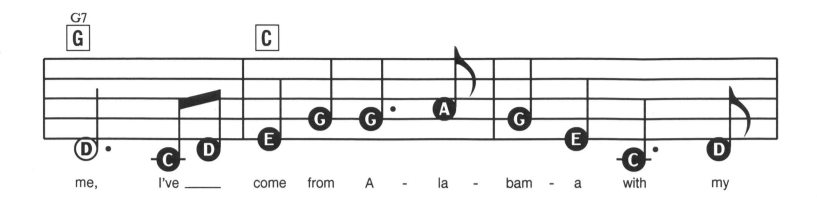

me, I've ____ come from A - la - bam - a with my

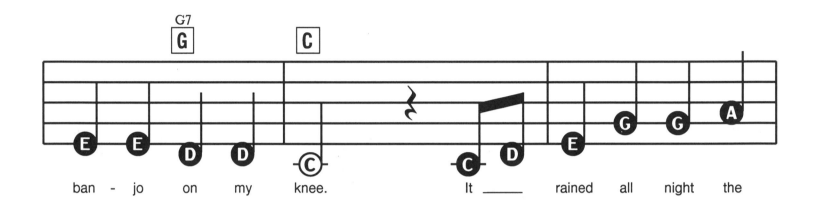

ban - jo on my knee. It ____ rained all night the

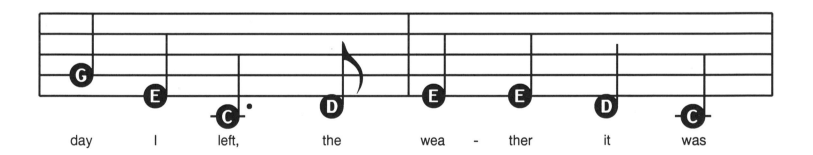

day I left, the wea - ther it was

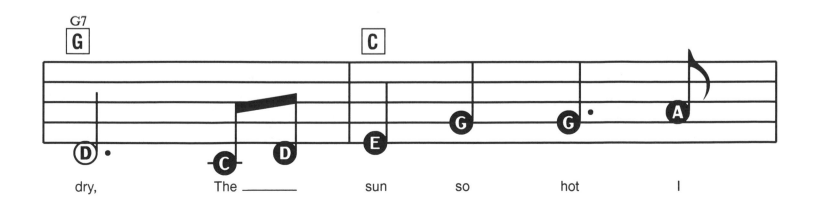

dry, The ____ sun so hot I

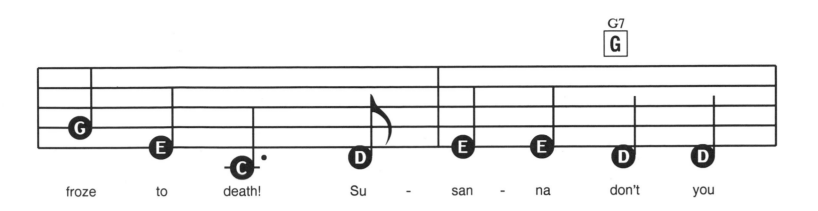

froze   to   death!   Su - san - na   don't   you

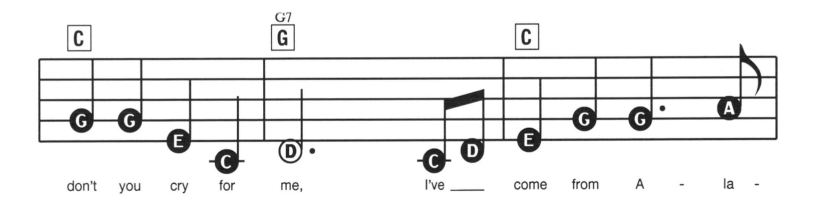

cry.   Oh!   Su - san - na,   Oh,

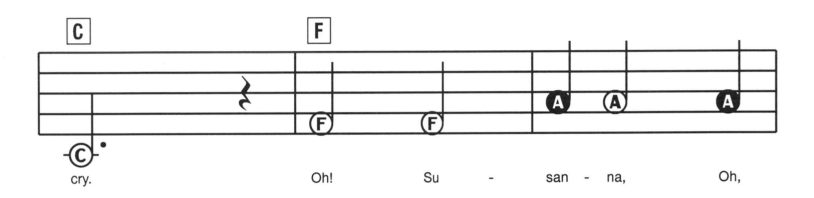

don't you cry for me,   I've ____ come from A - la -

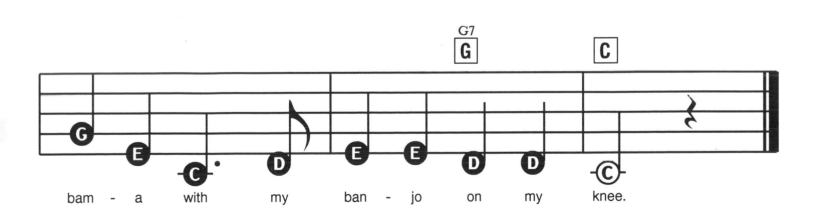

bam - a with my ban - jo on my knee.

Oh, Them Golden Slippers

Registration 7
Rhythm: Country

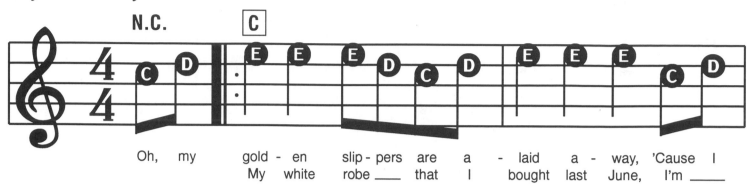

Oh, my gold - en slip - pers are a - laid a - way, 'Cause I
My white robe ___ that I bought last June, I'm ___

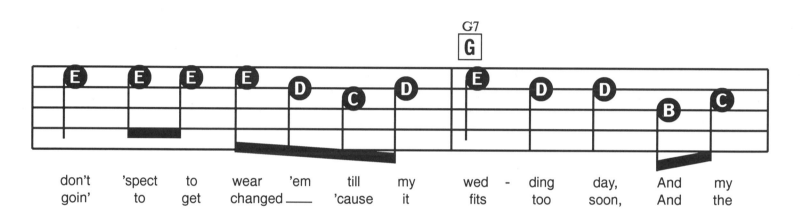

don't 'spect to wear 'em till my wed - ding day, And my
goin' 'spect to get changed ___ 'em 'cause it fits too soon, And the

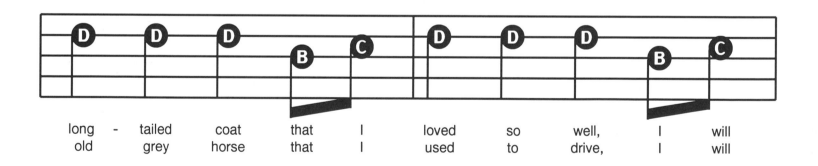

long - tailed coat that I loved so well, I will
old grey horse that I used to drive, I will

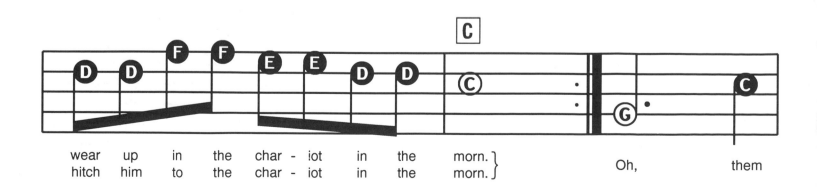

wear up in the char - iot in the morn.⎫
hitch him to the char - iot in the morn.⎭
Oh, them

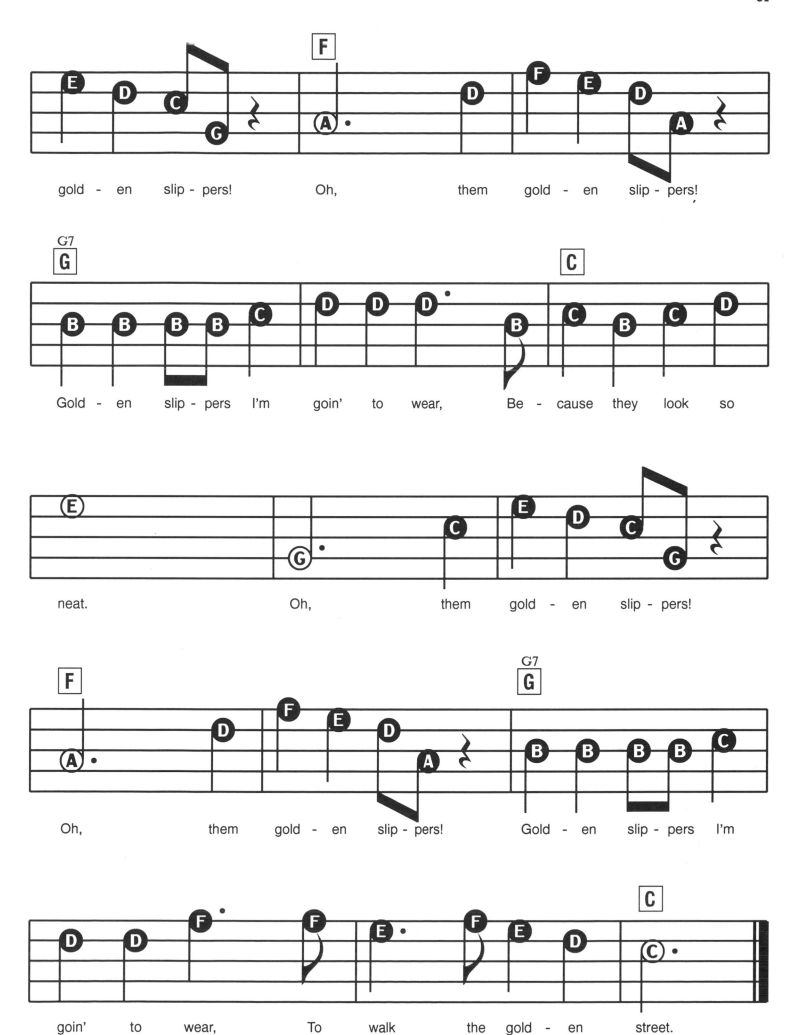

gold - en slip-pers! Oh, them gold - en slip - pers!

Gold - en slip - pers I'm goin' to wear, Be - cause they look so

neat. Oh, them gold - en slip - pers!

Oh, them gold - en slip - pers! Gold - en slip - pers I'm

goin' to wear, To walk the gold - en street.

On Top Of Old Smoky

Registration 1
Rhythm: Waltz

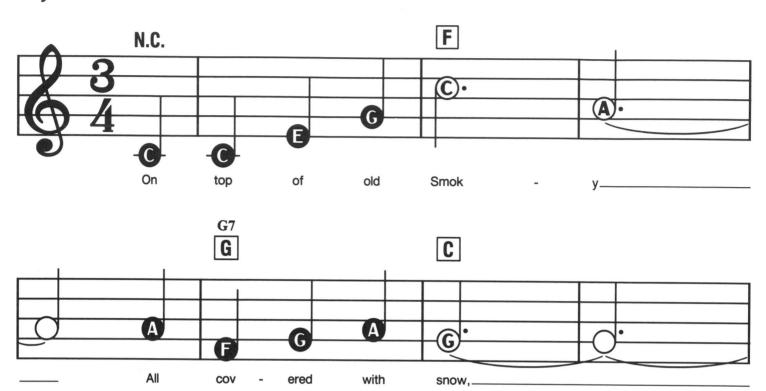

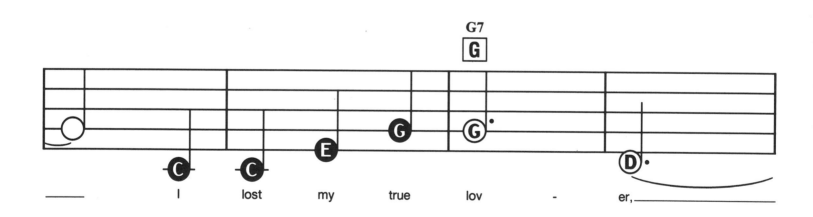

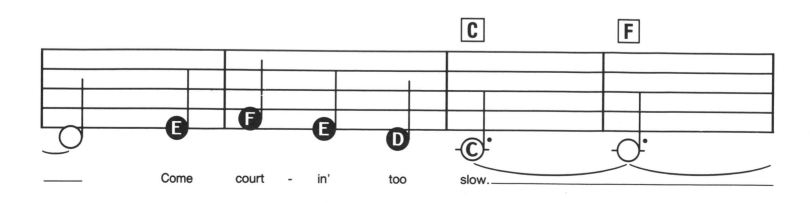

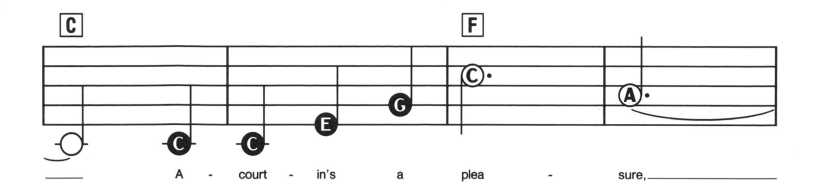

A - court - in's a plea - sure,_____

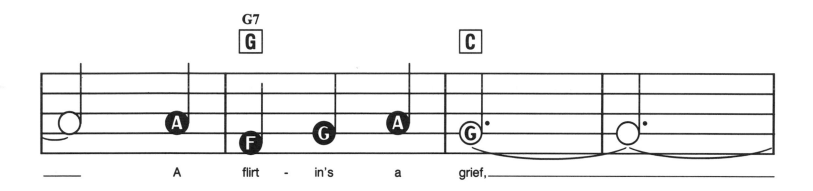

A flirt - in's a grief,_____

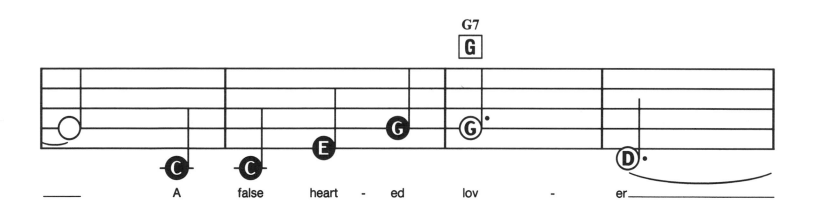

A false heart - ed lov - er_____

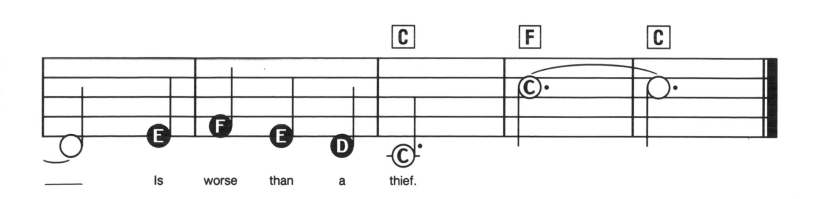

Is worse than a thief.

Over The Waves

Registration 3
Rhythm: Waltz

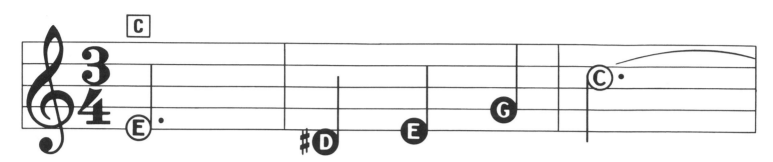

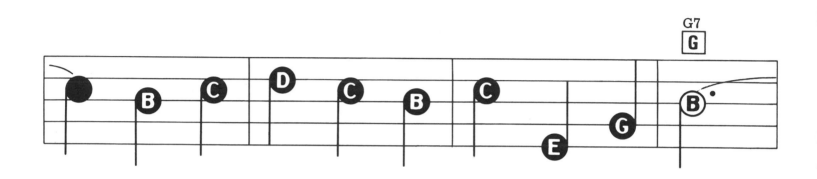

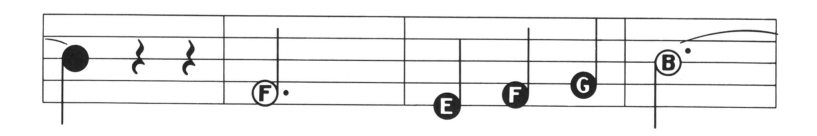

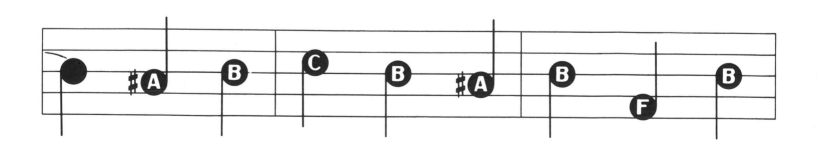

65

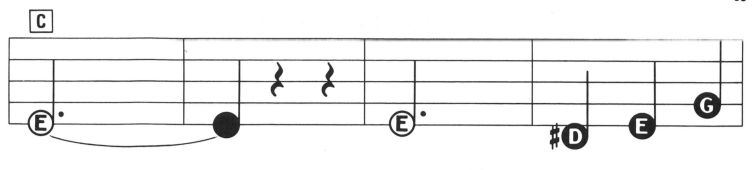

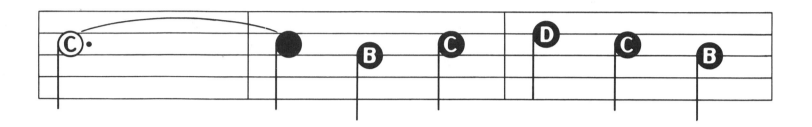

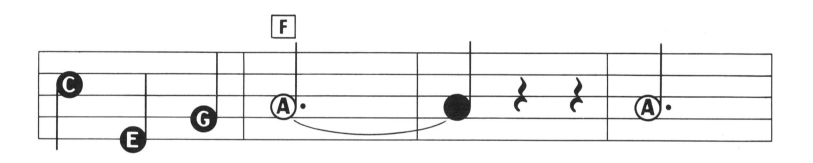

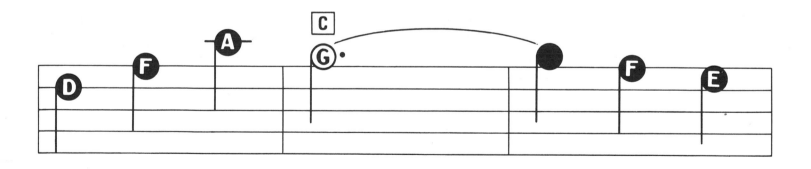

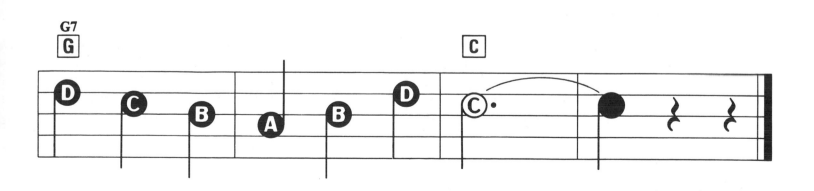

Red River Valley

Registration 4
Rhythm: Country

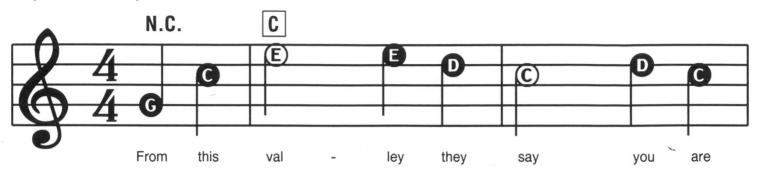

From this val - ley they say you are

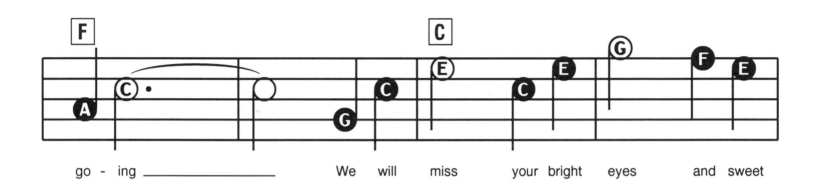

go - ing _____ We will miss your bright eyes and sweet

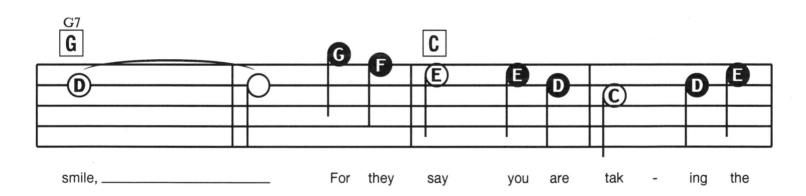

smile, _____ For they say you are tak - ing the

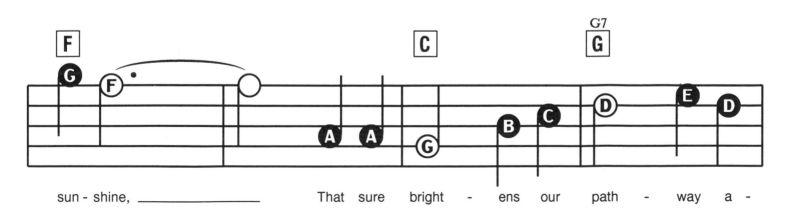

sun - shine, _____ That sure bright - ens our path - way a -

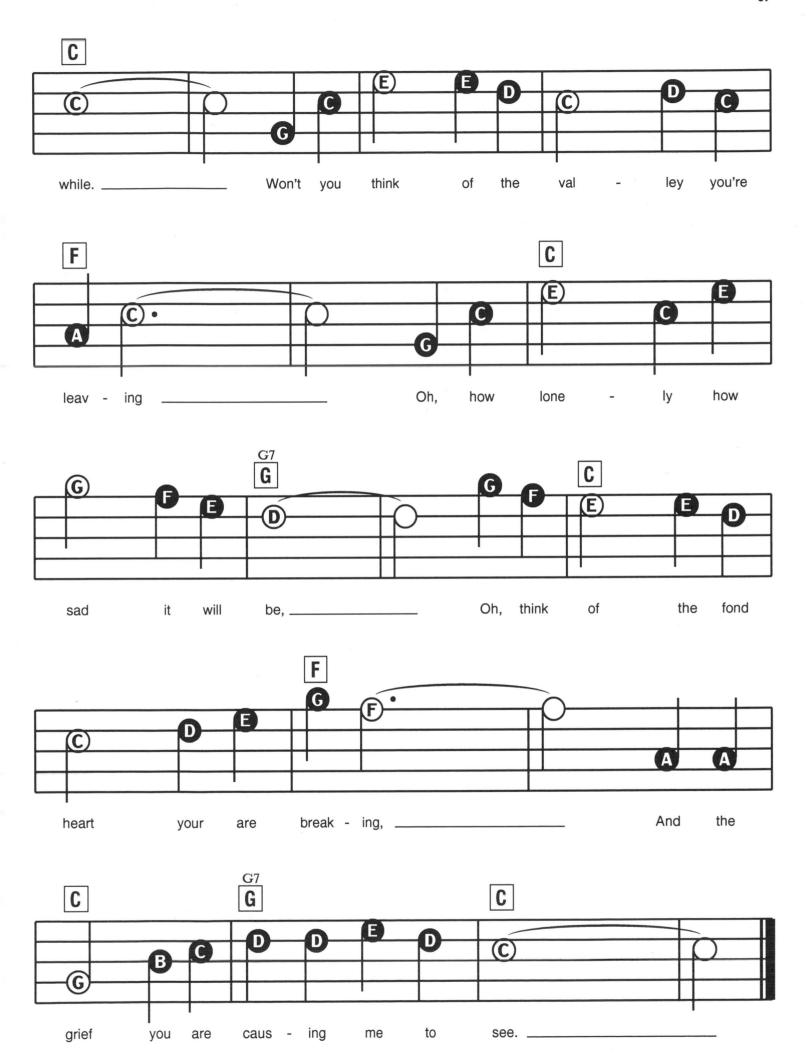

Shenandoah

Registration 3
Rhythm: Rock or Pops

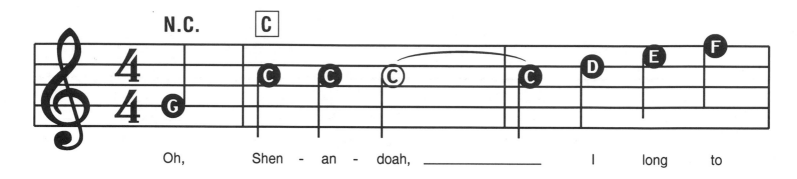

Oh,   Shen - an - doah, _____ I   long   to

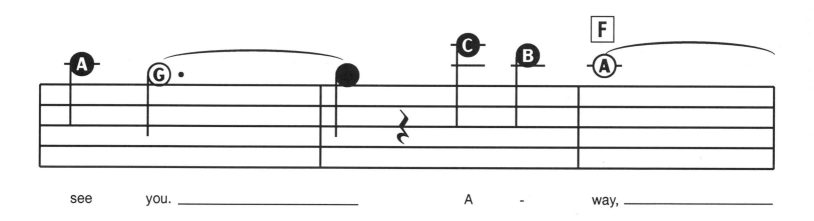

see   you. _____ A - way, _____

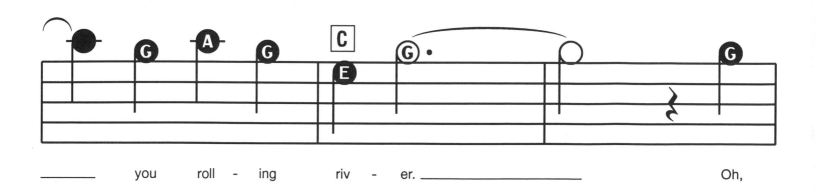

_____ you roll - ing riv - er. _____ Oh,

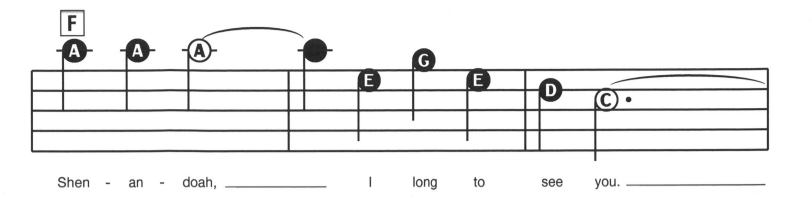

Shen - an - doah, _____ I long to see you. _____

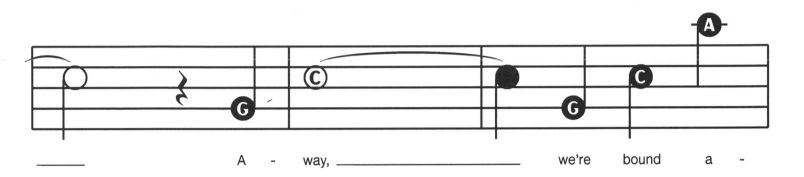

_____ A - way, _____ we're bound a -

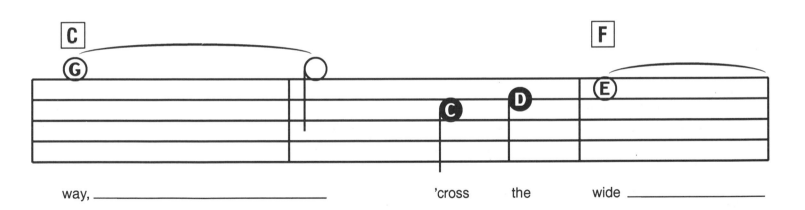

way, _____ 'cross the wide _____

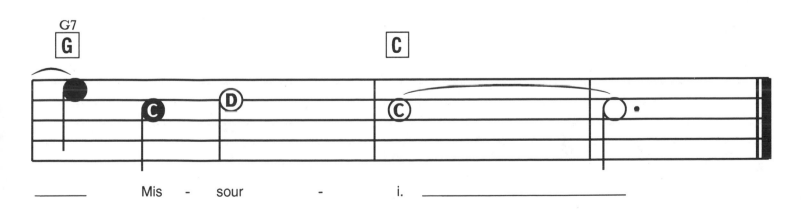

_____ Mis - sour - i. _____

Ta-Ra-Ra-Boom-De-Ay

Registration 5
Rhythm: March

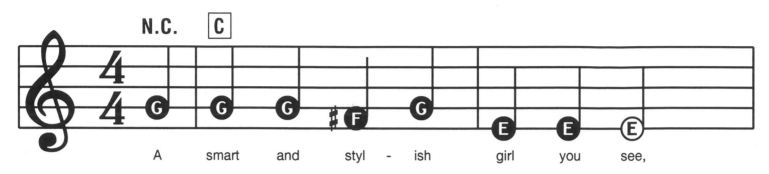

A smart and styl - ish girl you see,

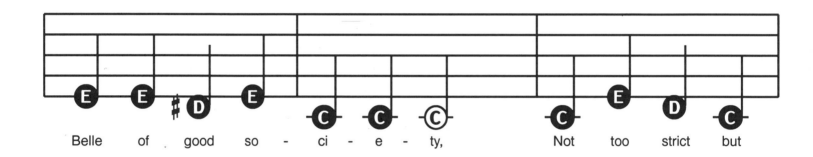

Belle of good so - ci - e - ty, Not too strict but

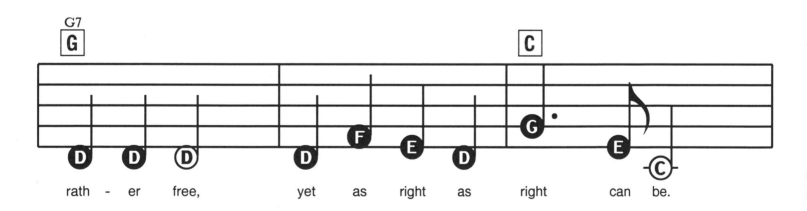

rath - er free, yet as right as right can be.

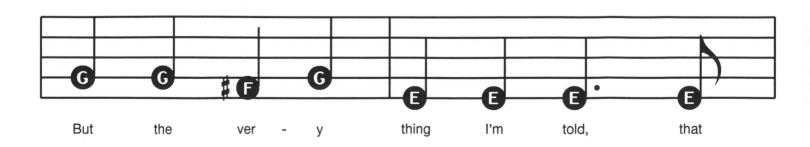

But the ver - y thing I'm told, that

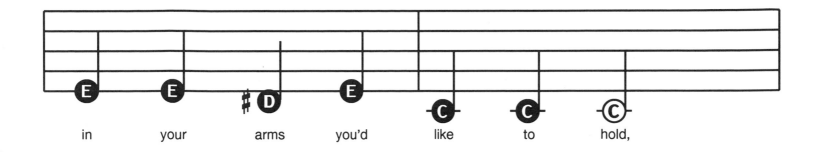

in your arms you'd like to hold,

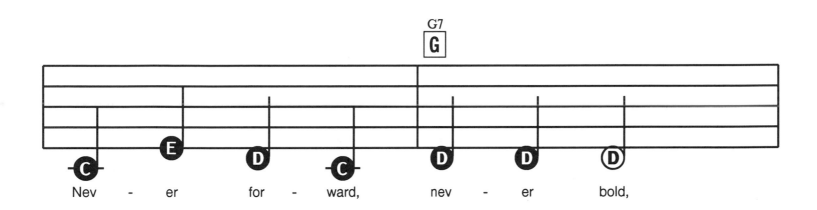

G7
Nev - er for - ward, nev - er bold,

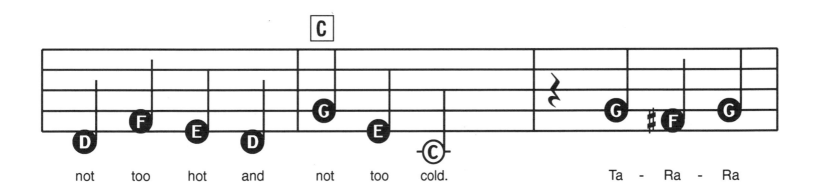

C
not too hot and not too cold. Ta - Ra - Ra

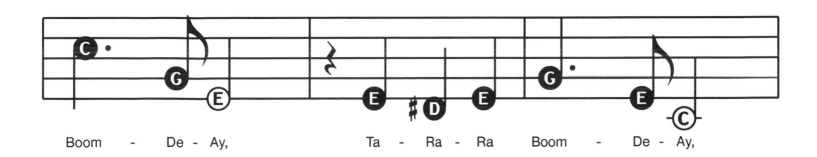

Boom - De - Ay, Ta - Ra - Ra Boom - De - Ay,

72

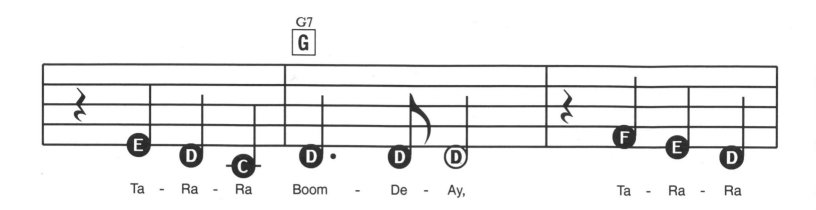

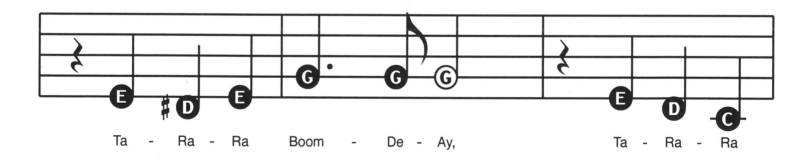

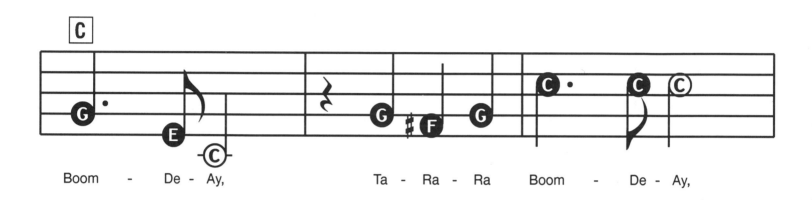

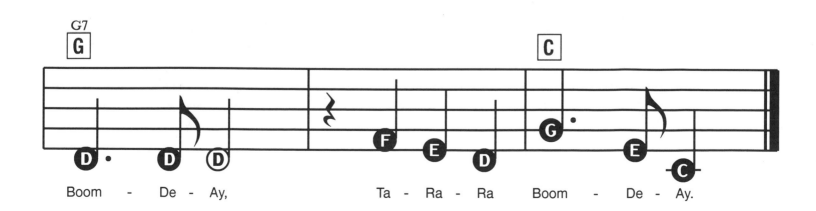

Wabash Cannon Ball

Registration 5
Rhythm: Country or March

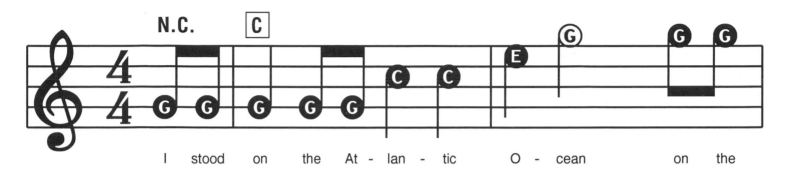

I stood on the At - lan - tic O - cean on the

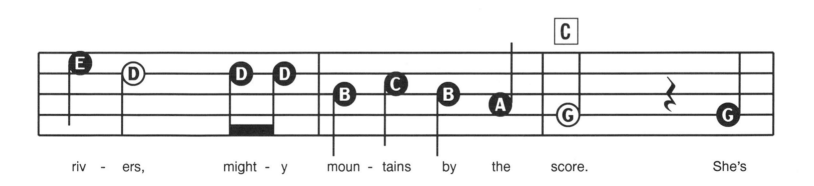

wide Pa - ci - fic shore, saw the queen of flow - ing

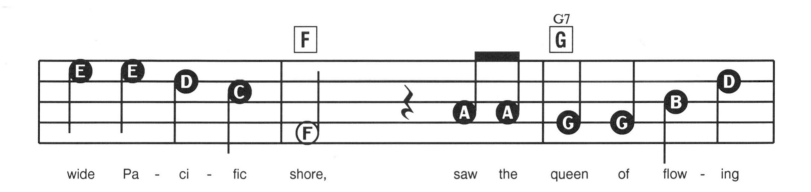

riv - ers, might - y moun - tains by the score. She's

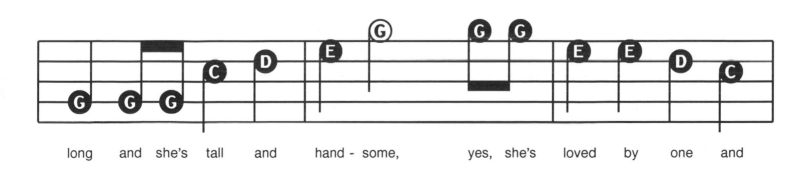

long and she's tall and hand - some, yes, she's loved by one and

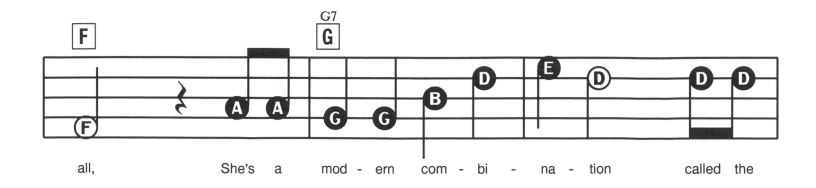

all, She's a mod - ern com - bi - na - tion called the

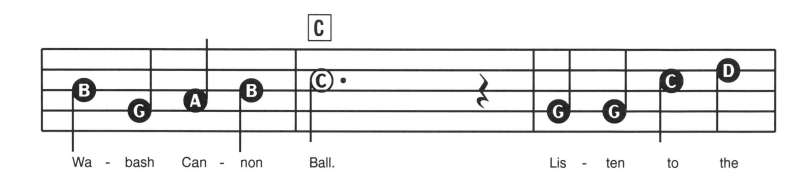

Wa - bash Can - non Ball. Lis - ten to the

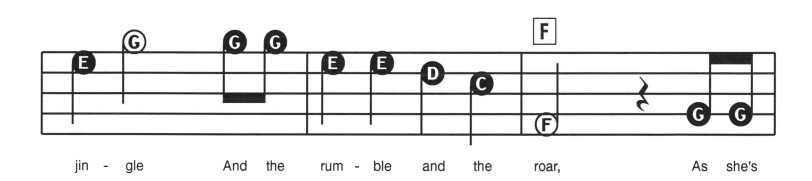

jin - gle And the rum - ble and the roar, As she's

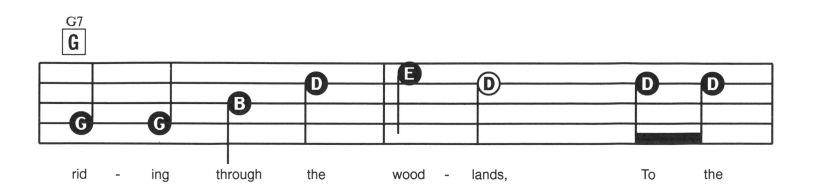

rid - ing through the wood - lands, To the

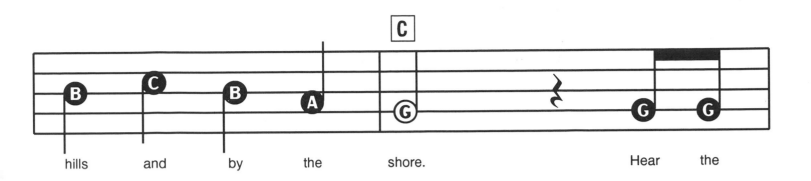

hills   and   by   the   shore.   Hear   the

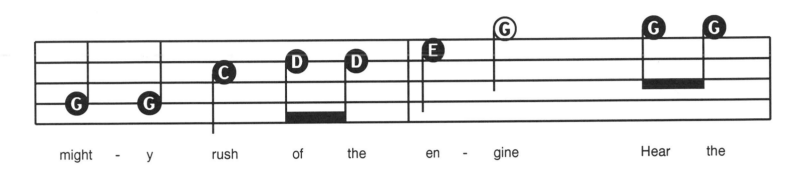

might - y   rush   of   the   en - gine   Hear   the

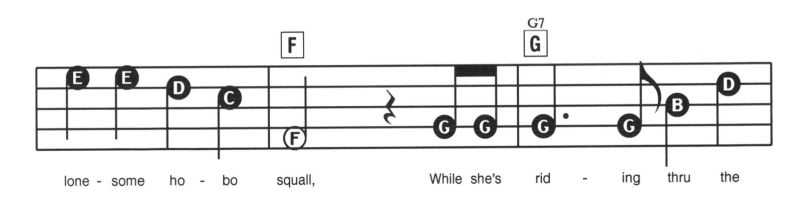

lone - some   ho - bo   squall,   While   she's   rid - ing   thru   the

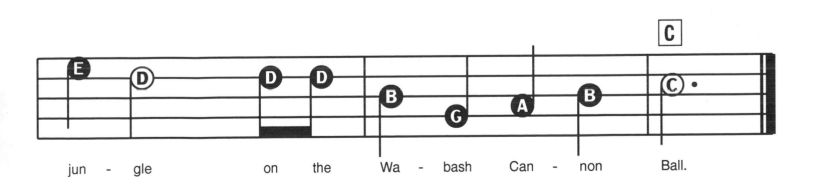

jun - gle   on   the   Wa - bash   Can - non   Ball.

Yankee Doodle

Registration 9
Rhythm: March

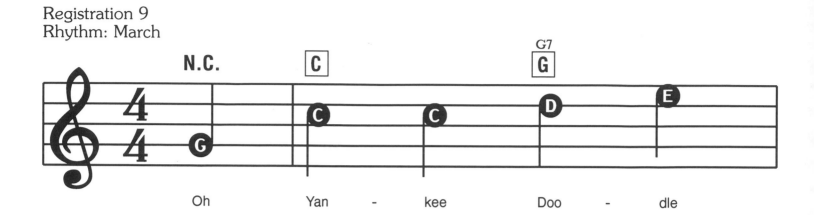

Oh   Yan - kee   Doo - dle

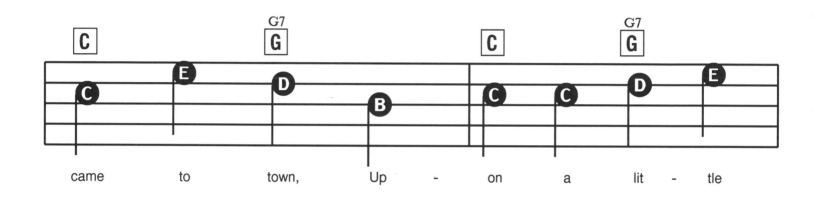

came   to   town,   Up - on   a   lit - tle

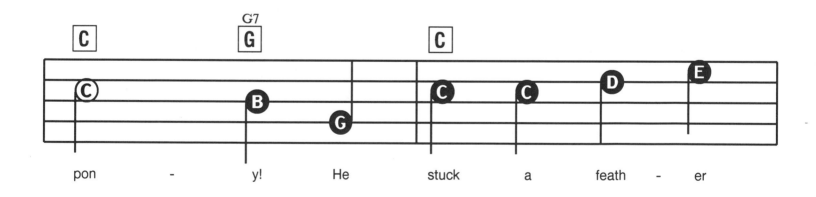

pon - y!   He   stuck   a   feath - er

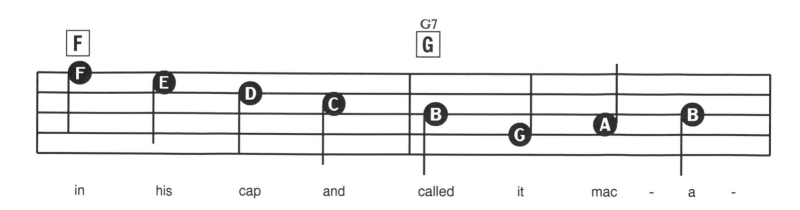

in   his   cap   and   called   it   mac - a -

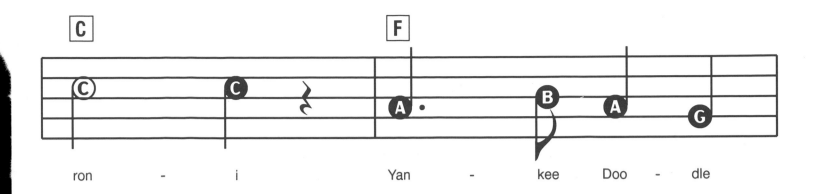

ron - i Yan - kee Doo - dle

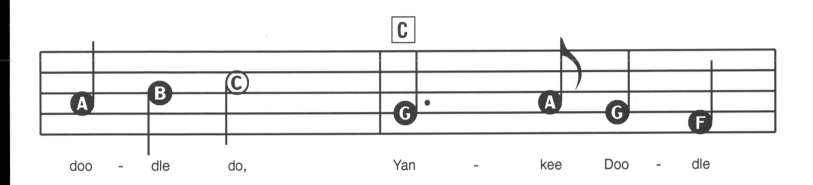

doo - dle do, Yan - kee Doo - dle

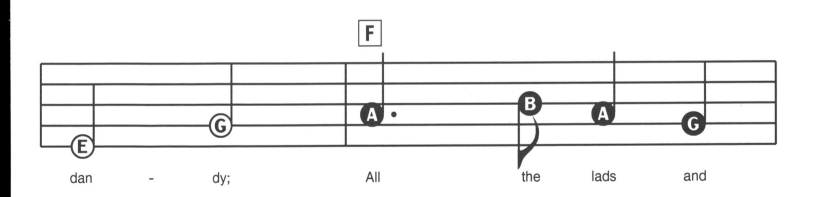

dan - dy; All the lads and

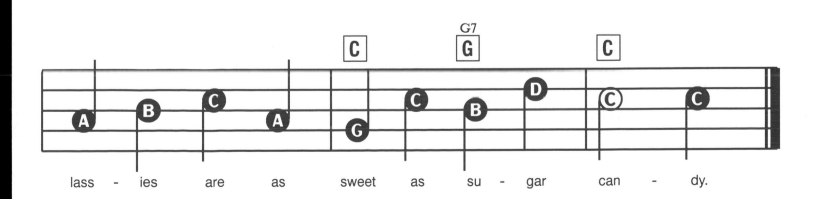

lass - ies are as sweet as su - gar can - dy.

Yellow Rose Of Texas

Registration 3
Rhythm: March

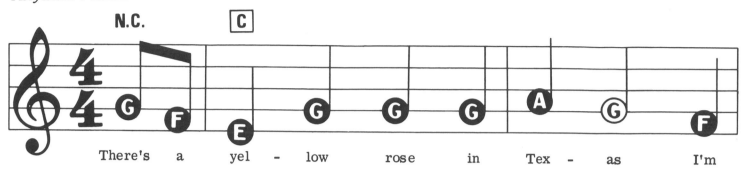

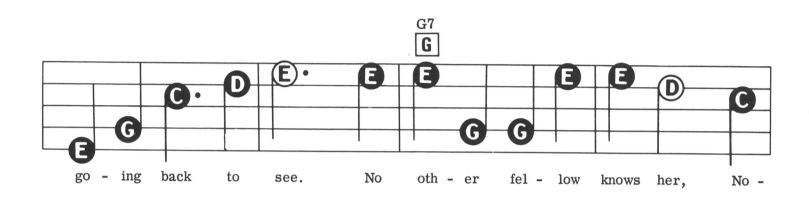

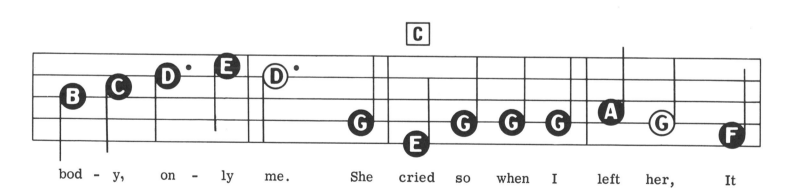

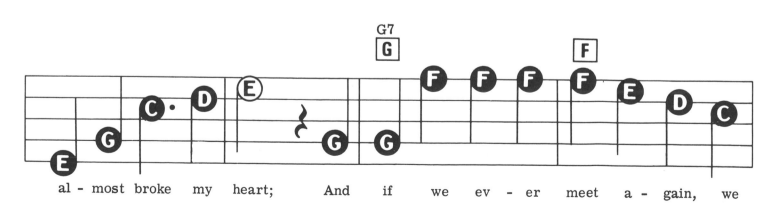

nev - er more shall part.   She's the sweet-est rose of col - or this

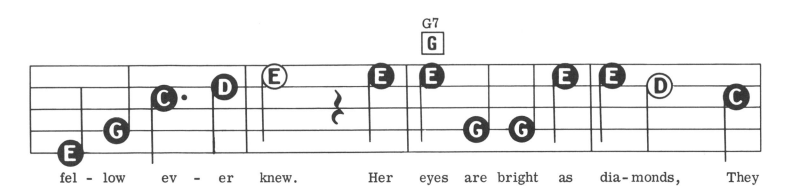

fel - low ev - er knew.   Her eyes are bright as dia-monds,   They

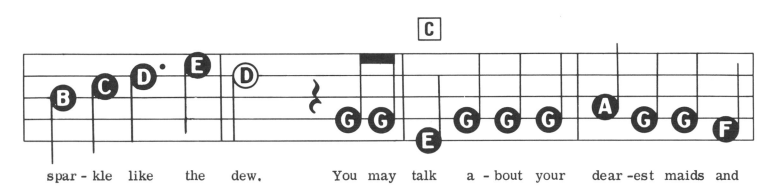

spar - kle like the dew.   You may talk a - bout your dear -est maids and

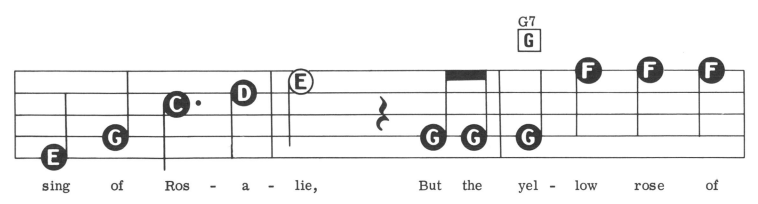

sing of Ros - a - lie,   But the yel - low rose of

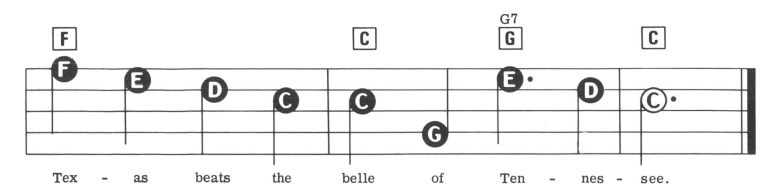

Tex - as beats the belle of Ten - nes - see.

When The Saints Go Marching In

Registration 2
Rhythm: Swing

Negro spiritual

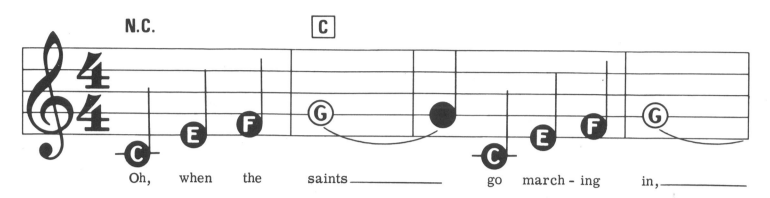

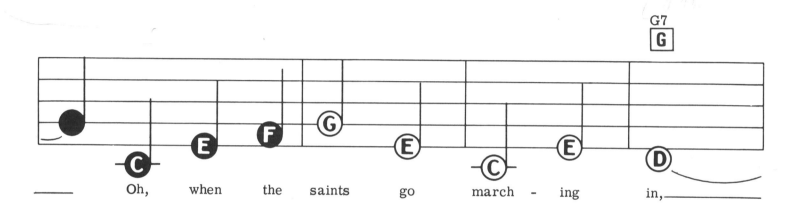

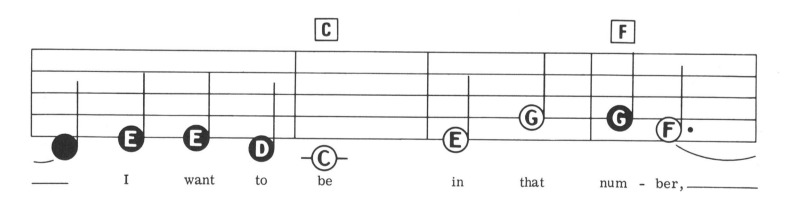

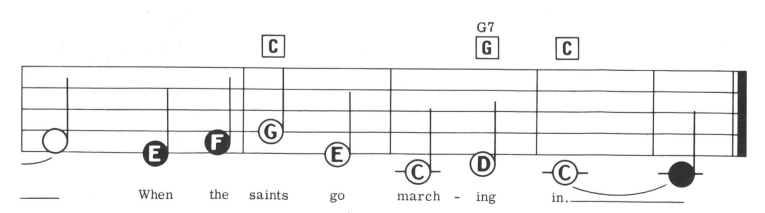